Wooden Toys

Didier Carpentier

Joël Bachelet

EP PUBLISHING LIMITED

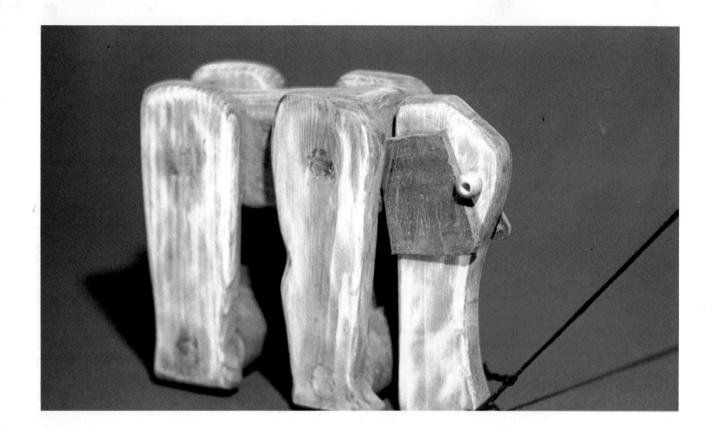

Originally published in France under the title *Jouets en bois*
Copyright © 1979 Dessain et Tolra

Design and photography by the authors

Translated by A. F. Hartley and P. Picot

English edition copyright © 1982 EP Publishing Limited

Published by EP Publishing Limited, Bradford Road, East
Ardsley, Wakefield, West Yorkshire, WF3 2JN, England

Phototypeset in England by
CTL Computer Typesetters, Leeds

Printed and bound in Italy

ISBN 0 7158 0785 4

Contents

Introduction

Everyone has dreamt, at one time or another, of making one of these splendid wooden toys, endlessly fascinating to a child, from the rocking-horse – glorious figure of a golden age – to those little wooden puppets which express the emotions and marvels of childhood.

In this book we have tried to recreate this golden age, enabling those who love the beauty of wood to make wooden toys for themselves according to their ability and imagination, and using simple tools and techniques.

It is not by chance that the tradition of wooden toys has survived the industrial era of plastics and is still highly rated by a good number of people. Wood has remained the most popular material for making everyday objects because of its irreplaceable qualities and strength, safety, warmth and beauty; it is a living material on a human scale.

There are many ways of working with wood: from a block, a board, mouldings, modules. In this book, we will not be concentrating on wood carving from a block, as this technique is really closer to sculpture. We will use it only for simple objects. For the rest, we have endeavoured to show you methods which are better suited to basic tools.

Before the instructions for each toy we have provided a materials list. In practically all cases, an excess of material is specified to allow for sawing, planing and finishing. Where the part is difficult to hold while it is being shaped, a little extra is allowed for gripping in the vice. This is why the sizes given in the lists of materials required are not always exactly the same as those specified for the finished parts. All the dimensions are in millimetres or metres.

In several models, small components are not listed separately; these are to be made from off-cuts from the larger pieces.

The first part of the book will deal with the techniques used in making the wooden toys shown in the second part.

If you are not used to working with wood, we advise you to start with simple models, trying to improve your technique as you go along. When you have acquired a certain skill, you will be able to make your own wooden toys, finding your inspiration in the numerous examples shown in this book.

Unfinished wood, painted wood, blocks or lengths of wood, waste wood – whichever you use, you will soon realise that woodworking is not an impossibly difficult craft. Anyone can do it, and it offers the advantage of combining graphic expression (designs and patterns) with plastic expression (3-dimensional creation).

Tools

The basic equipment for working sheets or lengths of wood consists of a few traditional tools which can be found in any handyman's standard kit. We will be using the most common ones which should enable you to carry out most types of woodwork. (In a few cases more advanced tools will be specified.) There are several different categories:

Marking tools

Marking is usually done using a well-sharpened pencil, a marking-knife, a pair of compasses, a bevel square, and a marking gauge. You will also need a graduated ruler and a tape-measure.

Boring tools

These include the gimlet (2 to 8 mm in diameter), the hand-drill, the bradawl, the power drill, and a brace. It is also necessary to have a set of twist bits (1 to 25 mm) or a set of centre-bits. The drills generally used for metalwork can sometimes be used in woodwork, but centring is more difficult. Using a bradawl to start the drill will help.

Cutting tools

Chisels and saws are the main cutting tools. These include the jig-saw for thick sheets; the general-purpose saw for cutting large straight panels; the tenon-saw for delicate jointing work and for work using the mitre-box; and the fret-saw for cutting curves.

Shaping tools

These include planes, rasps (half round, flat, round) and files (half round and triangular). Planes are used to square and to shave the sides of a piece of wood. Rasps are tempered steel tools with small teeth which remove wood quickly. Files differ from the rasps in their cutting edges. Their teeth are finer, giving a better finish.

Surforms are a cross between files and planes, with replaceable blades. They produce a smooth finish and are fast-cutting. There are three types: flat, round and "half-round" (actually an arc).

Other shaping tools include gouges, chisels (2 to 40 mm in width) and mortise chisels. They are used to shape a block of wood (notches, grooves, reliefs). The cutting edge of the chisels should be bevelled at 25°.

Tools used for the finishing of wood surfaces

Again, these include the gouges and firmer chisels used for carving designs. Poker work (pyrography) can also be used. Colouring wood is done using dyes or model paints (or lacquer for a better finish). A set of brushes is also useful, together with the appropriate solvents for cleaning them after use.

Brace and bits

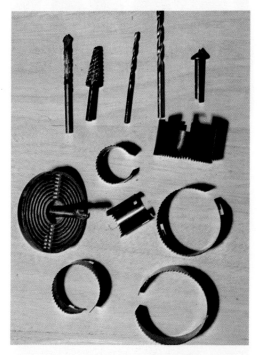

Countersinks, drills and expander bits

Files, chisels, gouges and drills

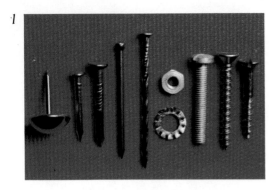

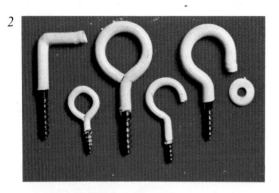

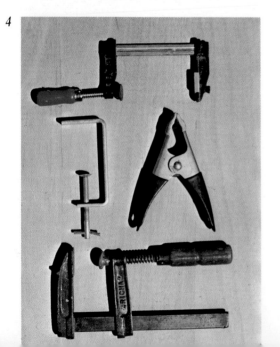

Assembly materials

Different tools and equipment are needed for each type of construction. Wood glues as well as fasteners are used.

Glues are divided into two categories: 'physical' glues (vinyl resins are the most useful) and chemical glues (formaldehyde, melamine etc.).

The 'physical' glues, such as white vinyl adhesive, are well suited for bonding light-coloured plywood. We advise against using a glue which dries in several layers because this shows that its talc content is too high and its vinyl content too low. Vinyl glues dry hard in 12 to 24 hours. Of this type, resin 'W' is best for general use. Strong glues are used for delicate jointing. Casein glues are well suited for woods such as red pine, teak or rosewood.

Contact adhesives (chemical glues) are used for laminated surfaces. They are ideal for bonding large areas. Clamping or screwing is unnecessary with this type of adhesive; in fact no adjustment is possible after contact has been made. The surfaces should thus be fitted dry first.

It will be useful to complete your tool-box with assorted fastenings which will enable you to join together most types of work. For this, buy a selection of tacks, veneer pins, lost-head nails (25 mm long), countersunk screws 15 to 30 mm long, nuts and bolts, as well as a set of screw eyes and cuphooks, hinges and staples, draw-pins the same diameter as the drill bits, a hammer, a pair of pliers, a screwdriver, a mallet and a palette knife.

Accessories

We also suggest a vice to hold the pieces of wood in position, and several clamps (thumb screw, G-clamps).

Basic workshop facilities, such as a shed or a corner of the garage, will make your job a lot easier, but a work-bench big enough to fit a vice and some clamps is sufficient. An old table would do, provided that it does not move or wobble, and that it is the correct height for comfortable working. Alternatively, many do-it-yourself shops sell fold-away metal work-benches with integral vice.

1. Brass chair nail, flat-headed nails, lost-head nail, screw nail, locking washer, nut, bolt, chipboard screw (self-tapping), wood screw 2. Cup hooks, eyelets and nylon washer 3. Draw-pin, rivet, split-pin 4. Different types of clamp

1

1. Different types of moulding
2. Shrinkage cracks in a section of wood
3. Beech   4. African hardwood

2

Materials

As wood is a living material, it does not have a uniform structure (unlike, for example, a block of metal). Therefore, it needs to be processed before being used – by conversion, which consists of cutting the log into boards (with the grain); by drying or seasoning, which consists of reducing the degree of moisture in the wood; and finally, by shaping. If the wood has been badly processed, a large number of faults may result, such as splitting, warping and cracking.

The timber industry deals with about a hundred different sorts of wood, but here we will be concentrating only on the types of wood suitable for toy making. Pine is particularly suitable for toys made from unfinished wood; beech, a pliable wood, can easily be bowed; birch is used to make flat articles which do not require a fine surface quality; balsa is used for light constructions; gaboon and ash lend themselves easily to carving and painting, though gaboon has a low resistance to stress; baboen is quite strong for its density; poplar can be glued or dyed without any problem (yet it is not easy to shape); alder is used for shaping toys from a block of wood; ilomba is of a pinkish colour and of a porous nature. You can also find veneered woods – usually oak or mahogany – but they are not available in a very wide range of sizes, and are very expensive.

3

Beech, pine, birch, balsa and gaboon are sold in shops in boards, lengths and mouldings. The toys selected in this book have been made from these already shaped and standardised elements.

The boards used are of one of three categories: thin sections 4–6–8–12 and 18 mm in thickness; 20–22–24–27–34–41–47 mm boards; and boards 54–60–68–72 mm (and then multiples of 6 mm, up to 108 mm).

4

1

2

3

Plywoods also come in various thicknesses: 3, 4, 6, 9, 12 mm etc. They include multi-ply, made from an odd number of sheets; blockboard, made of a central core of strips sandwiched between two outer sheets; and laminboard, made of narrow strips of wood glued together, similar to blockboard. The main characteristics of plywood are its lightness, strength and ability to remain flat.

With 12% moisture, the average density per sheet is dependent upon the species of wood: gaboon: 0.45 g/cm³; poplar: 0.50; mahogany: 0.55. A square metre of gaboon 10 mm thick weighs 4.5 kg, which amounts to about 15 kg for a standard sheet. Some parts can be cut from beams.

There are many mouldings and shaped strips. They are found in circular sections, often used for dowels, and in rectangular, square and curved sections. They can be in different sizes, their length being generally between 1 and 2 m.

Many other ready-to-use elements (beads, balls, cubes, rings, etc.) can be used in the making of wooden toys. Particle boards (e.g. chipboard) should not be used since their edges have to be filled in first. We strongly advise against using them since their coarse structure does not lend itself to precise sawing. Fibre boards (hardboard) should also be avoided, unless used as unstressed panels.

The choice of wood is important. In each case, it must be chosen according to the toys you want to make. Small parts should preferably be cut from medium hardwood, parts which need greater flexibility should be cut out of softwood. On the other hand, parts which are likely to become distorted should be cut out of hardwood, as well as those which will be part of a musical instrument (the bars of a xylophone, for instance).

The faults and imperfections in wood can sometimes be turned to decorative advantage. Try to match the grain of the wood and, as often as possible, to match the type of material with the characteristics of the toy to be made. If a part has an elongated shape, try to cut it in the direction of the grain. Apart from the aesthetic aspect (always a controversial subject), various technical considerations will narrow your choice. Indeed, the criterion of sturdiness should be of paramount importance.

Softwoods are generally more porous than hardwoods and therefore more difficult to paint. Several coats, starting with primer, are necessary to obtain a perfect, even finish.

The selection of woods shown here is not intended to be exhaustive, but may give a good idea of the variety available.

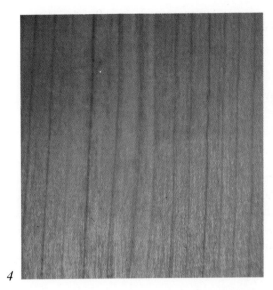

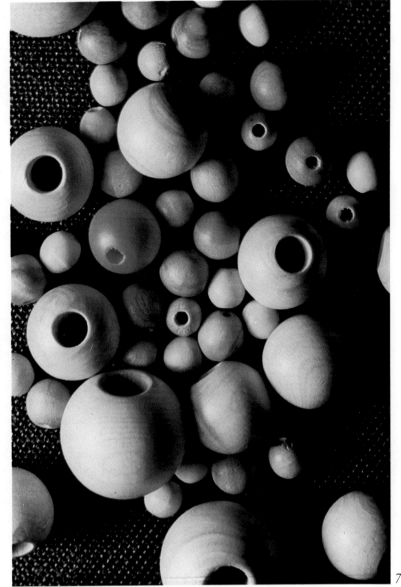

1. Gaboon   2. Ash.   3. Oak   4. Wild cherry
5. Walnut   6. White ash   7. Wooden beads

The structure of blockboard

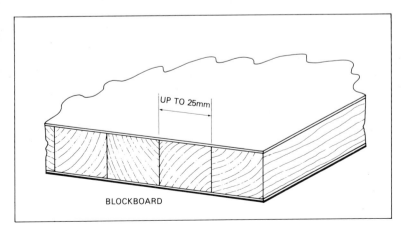

UP TO 25mm

BLOCKBOARD

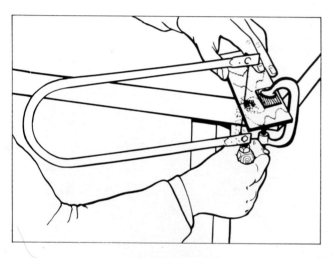

Notch made with a general-purpose saw

The fret-saw must be held vertical

Cutting dowel to length with a tenon-saw

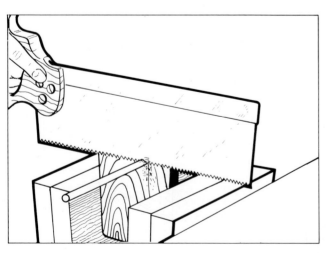

Construction

To make the toys shown in this book, you should follow carefully the instructions given below. Although these are not of a highly technical nature, great care must be taken at each of the different stages of the toys' construction.

Naturally, you need to know how to mark, saw, file, shape, drill countersink, glasspaper and fit in order to make these wooden toys. These techniques are essential and will be dealt with in the first part of this book; in the second part we will be concentrating on the details of each individual toy.

Marking

Try to be very accurate when marking, especially with the jointed puppets, for it is at this stage that many mistakes can be made which could prove disastrous later on in the construction. In order to avoid variations when cutting out, the toys are designed on a very simple scale with precise dimensions.

Designs with an irregular outline should be marked out on a flat surface. Thus it should be easier to enlarge them using the squared paper method or any other such system (pantograph, for example). The transfer of the design is done using tracing paper, the design side against the wood, so that it can be printed by simply rubbing with a burnisher or a brush handle. Your tracing paper should be fixed to the piece of wood with adhesive tape. In some cases, you can make a template out of stiff cardboard and transfer the pattern onto the wood using a pencil to outline the design. The design can be drawn on the cardboard either directly or using tracing paper. Use a pair of compasses to check the dimensions of identical segments.

Sawing

Sawing a length or a sheet of wood is always a delicate operation, even for simple parts. A good cut is dependent upon a straight blade and a steady stroke. As a rule, the edge should not require any more adjustment.

There are three main types of cut: straight, convex and concave. Straight cuts are made using a general-purpose saw or a tenon-saw, according to the thickness of the wood. Convex cuts are made with a compass-saw; and concave cuts are made with a pad-saw. If the wood is thin, a fret-saw can be used for convex or concave cuts. Thick boards should be cut using a jig-saw (a machine saw) or a suitable hand-saw, keeping as near as possible to the outline of the design by successive cuts and by rounding off the angles, using a file or surform.

As a rule, the size of the teeth depends on the size of the piece of wood to be sawn. For example, if the teeth are too long they might rip the wood, especially in the case of plywood. The saw must be held firmly but not too tightly. Cut a small notch by an initial backward stroke, as a guide for the first saw strokes. To allow for finishing, care should be taken always to saw on the waste side of the line. In this way, you can carefully plane or file away the excess wood. The general-purpose saw is usually held at 45°. At the end of the cut, it should be held vertically to avoid splintering the wood.

Whenever possible, it is best to hold the wood firmly in position on your work table before sawing. For this, use a clamp and place some small blocks of waste wood between the piece of wood to be cut and the clamp face, in order to protect the material.

To saw lengths without any problem using a tenon-saw, it is best to use a mitre-box in order to cut small sections at 90° or 45°. It is also advisable to hold the mitre-box in position.

Sharpening the teeth is a very skilled job, best left to an expert. It is done using a saw file, which is triangular in section. Craftsmen usually apply paraffin or soap to the blade to facilitate sharpening.

Filing

After being cut, the parts will need to be trimmed, using a rasp or surform for large pieces and a file for small ones. This operation is essential since it trims all the splinters and imperfections of the cutting. Trim the rough edges towards the inner face of the sheet in order to avoid new splinters. The file or rasp strokes should be angled slightly, according to the plane of the surface to be trimmed.

Round (rat's-tail) files are particularly useful for smoothing tight radii and small circular holes. The bigger round files are used to file large concave curves. Trimming the edges with a plane requires a perfectly sharpened blade. The cutting edge should be accurately perpendicular to the sides of the plane. It should be bevelled at 25° and sharpened at 30°.

Sawing with a mitre box

Planing edges

Finishing with a round and a flat file

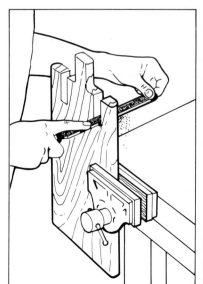
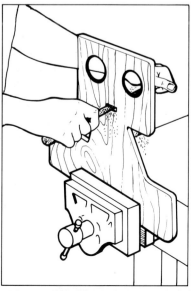

1

2

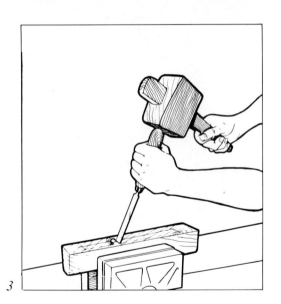

3

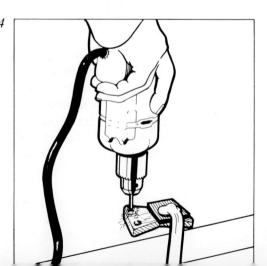

4

Sanding

After being filed, the edges should be sanded with abrasive papers of different grit numbers (start with a coarse one, progress to a medium, and end with a fine). Preferably, use a power sander for large areas, although it may be necessary to paint them because of the marks left on the wood. The disc should be held at an angle of 20°. To obtain a perfectly smooth surface, it is advisable to wet the wood slightly after sanding in order to lift the cells of the wood. Another quick sanding when the wood is dry again should eliminate irregularities completely. Where possible use glasspaper on a cork block.

Shaping

You may have to make some parts of the toys from a solid block of wood. For that, you must shape the part required with a plane. Cutting is done using a firmer or bevelled-edge chisel or a gouge. The chisel is mainly used to remove faults and to stop splits. The rasp is used once more for trimming and eliminating all the imperfections.

Milling

Milling-cutters and rasps can be fitted to any power drill. They are quick and accurate to use for finishing.

Milling-cutters enable you to make all sorts of mouldings. However, they require considerable skill and experience, and most amateur woodworkers will prefer to buy ready-moulded wood as required.

Files are used for the fine finish of a block of wood, plywood or laminated wood.

Drilling

To bore a perfectly vertical hole can sometimes be difficult. Here again, the correct position of the tool is vital. After deciding the exact position of the hole, start by drilling with a bradawl, a hand-drill or a gimlet. This first hole should be big enough for the bit of the power drill or the brace to bite deep into the wood and, most important, not to slide away. To make sure you are holding the drill vertically, use a small set square or a right-angled piece of wood. To drill with the power drill or brace, it is best to protect your work bench with a block placed under the hole.

Moreover, we advise you to practise drilling a few holes in waste wood in order to gain expertise. To make things easier, it is advisable to clamp the piece of wood whenever possible. With the power drill, holes are always made from the outer face of the boards. Drilling is stopped when the bit has gone through. The hole is then finished by drilling it again from the other side in order to remove any splinters caused by the first drilling.

Drill at low speed – 900 revs per minute. To drill a hole into – but not through – a piece of wood, you should use a stop equal to the difference between the length of the bit and the depth of the hole to be drilled. You can also make small slots by moving the drill horizontally. Oval holes are also made in this way.

Fitting during assembly

It is impossible to write about woodworking without mentioning fitting. This is a very delicate operation which often makes you wonder whether the wood has a mind of its own! Imagine your dismay when, after spending a whole day in your workshop, you find that one of the holes is too small, off-centre or too large. But don't despair – there are remedies.

First case: the hole is too small. The first solution consists of widening the hole by re-drilling or using a small round file in order to enlarge evenly the diameter of the hole. The second solution is to reduce the diameter of the dowel to fit the size of the hole, using a flat file.

Second case: the hole is off-centre. In this case, too, the inner edge of the hole should be filed in order to find the right position. A wedge is then inserted into the hole to compensate for the looseness. If the hole is badly off-line, plug it and re-drill.

Third case: the hole is too large. If fitting is made impossible because the dowel is too loose in the hole, the hole should again be plugged and the block re-drilled; or it may be possible to fit a larger dowel.

In the case of articulated toys, careful fitting is essential to obtain a perfect symmetry of the segments between the axles. For a free axle you should leave a gap of 1 or 2 mm in the housing according to the size of the part. Mortises and tenons are fitted using chisel and file. After each positioning, ensure a good fit by filing the part gradually.

Joining

Many types of joints are possible using open slots, glue, nuts and bolts, rivets, nails, mortises and tenons, draw-pins, wood screws, and clevis pins with split pins.

The open slot joint is one of the simplest. It entails making a slot with a saw in each of the parts, taking into account their length, and fitting them into each other. It is well suited for collapsible units, but requires great accuracy.

Mortise and tenon joints are renowned for their robustness. Very often they need to be glued in place. This technique consists of fitting one or several tenons, cut out with a saw, into a slot called a mortise. Tenons can be either single or double. Mortise and tenon joints are suitable for constructing frames and inserting rails (cross-pieces).

Joining with glue has the advantage of being less noticeable than metal fastenings. It is recommended for the permanent joining of

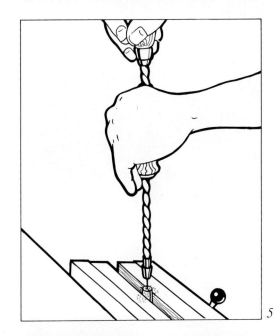

5

6

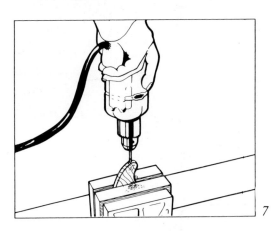

7

1. Sanding a flat area 2. Finishing with glass paper 3. Making a mortise with a mortise chisel. 4. Countersinking 5. Drilling a small hole with a hand-drill 6. Drilling a circular housing. Note the stop-mark on the bit to define the depth of drilling 7. When drilling a narrow section, grip the sides firmly in the vice

13

1

relatively small parts or joints which do not require to move. It is also used for joining pieces which slot together or mortise and tenon joints.

Nuts and bolts enable you to join two sheets which sandwich other parts between them. You need to drill a hole equal to the size of the bolt. Nothing must prevent it from going through cleanly.

Rivets or clevis pins and split pins are used mainly for jointed toys. In this case, too, holes need to be drilled. Another way of joining parts together is by using a dowel fixed at both ends by two small nails.

Nails are one of the most common means of joining. They are used for panels or boxes. The major drawback is that they show and can become dangerous if the toy comes apart.

The draw-pin joint is recommended for collapsible toys. It is used to hold together parts which fit through each other, using slightly tapered draw-pins inserted into holes drilled in one of the parts.

Wood-screws are used chiefly for screwing flat pieces together, which can be subsequently dismantled.

2

3

4

1. Assembling with glued dowel 2. Assembling with unglued dowel 3. Attachment for draw-string made with a staple 4. Assembling with a draw-pin

5. *Clamping parts which are being glued; hardwood blocks should be placed between the clamp head and the surface of the model to avoid damage and increase grip*   6. *Open-ended mortise*   7. *Mortise and tenon.*   8. *Rebate in multi-ply*

Finishing the surfaces

1. *Making a groove with a gouge*
2. *Varnishing   3. Stain-bath*
4. *Applying sealant with a spatula*
5. *Decorating with enamels*
6. *Decorating with coloured
adhesive film*

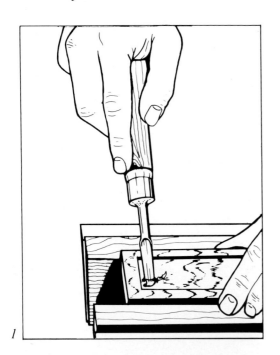

1

2

The finishing processes also include ways of decorating the wood. There are two kinds of process: those which give relief to the surface (by scoring, sanding, chiselling, scorching or engraving) and those which are basically pictorial and involve line-drawings or colour (painting, varnishing, drawing, etc.). The second group of processes will benefit from a small amount of preparation to avoid any slips.

Carving

This term refers to the technique which consists of giving relief to a surface. Although it is a very attractive technique, it is best to use it only for very simple work, such as the eyes and mouth of a figure. You will need a set of fine gouges and narrow chisels. Small holes can be bored using a bradawl. Three main types of groove are used in carving a relief: the V cut; grooves with a single vertical cut; and rounded grooves.

Engraving

This technique is somewhat similar to the one which has been used for centuries to engrave wood. Here the technique is used to decorate panels. The groove is done using a V-shape gouge or a skew chisel. The chisel is used for cutting the wood obliquely in order to dig in a V-shape groove along the outline of the design. There are other methods of engraving which enable you, at very low cost, to obtain all sorts of grooves. One of these is the simple method of overlapping different kinds of groove by marking the wood with straight lines (using chisels or mortise chisels) and curves (using rounded gouges or chisels).

Clear varnishes

Before varnishing, the wood must be sanded and cleaned using turpentine or linseed oil, according to the type of varnish used. Then the surface to be varnished must be sanded again.

There are as many types of varnish as there are brands. It is easiest to buy a small tin of polyurethane varnish for indoor toys, or yacht varnish for toys used mainly outdoors.

Coloured varnishes

If the wood is to be stained and if this has not been done at the finishing stage, you will have to use a coloured varnish. Finish off with an ordinary varnish. The purpose of varnishing is to protect the wood against dirt and the action of air and moisture, and to give it the required finish (gloss or matt).

Dyes

Wood may be dyed with spirit-based dyes or water-soluble dyes. Spirit dyes are expensive but do not raise the grain of the wood; water dyes are much cheaper but do raise the grain: the wood must be glasspapered down when dry and a second coat of dye applied. There are two methods of dyeing wood: soaking, which consists of dipping the piece of wood in a warm bath in which the dye has been dissolved; and applying the dye with a rag or a brush, which uses less dye, although the dye does not penetrate the wood as much as with soaking.

Wood imitations

Nowadays, with the introduction of new products, a piece of wood can be stained and coloured to resemble any other species of wood. These products are in fact dyes which have been made to match any sort of wood. Therefore you can stain your wood to look like ebony, mahogany, red pine, etc. For this you should choose a light-coloured wood, such as ash.

Applying lacquers and paints with a brush

Good preparation is essential before applying paints or lacquers to models. The best preparation, particularly when applying vinyl-based paints to large areas, is to coat the wood with a sealer. If this is not done, you will have to apply several coats of paint to cover the whole surface.

It is not advisable to paint panels which are too thin (because of the risk of warping) or on resinous wood (lack of adhesion). Drying time varies between thirty minutes and four hours, according to the paint used.

Waxing

Wooden objects can be waxed in different ways. The following method is particularly well suited for wooden toys.

After having dyed the wood to its chosen colour, rub it down if necessary with flour-paper or very fine glasspaper (no. 00). Apply a beeswax-based polish or a proprietory furniture wax (plain or coloured). Finally, buff with a dry duster or with a lambswool buff fixed in a hand-held power drill.

3

4

5

6

Coloured spinning top

Materials required

1 square of 6 mm plywood 60 × 60 mm
105 mm length of 6-mm diameter dowel rod

It is not so much the cutting out as the painting which makes this spinning top difficult to make, since although the cutting of the parts is not very complicated, the distribution of the colours is a delicate operation.

The spinning top is made of two sections. The first is a disc (55 mm diameter) cut out of a flat board 6 mm thick. The disc should be absolutely even, so glasspaper the edges carefully. The central hole must be positioned with great care. The second section is an axle 100 mm long and 6 mm in diameter. It is given a round point at one end and fitted tightly into the disc about 35 mm from the rounded end. The visual effect when the top is spinning, caused by the slowness of communication between the eye and the brain, cannot be achieved unless the colours are positioned perfectly. Therefore, try to keep to the design shown here (both colours and proportions) if you want to obtain the best effect from your spinning top. The seven colours used are the colours of the spectrum, i.e. red, orange, lemon yellow, green, light blue, indigo and violet. Each colour figures twice, forming two diametrically opposed halves.

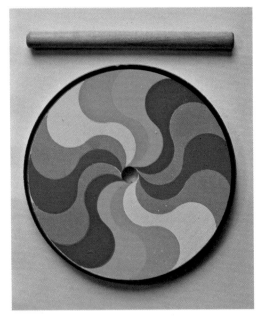

Colour distribution

The spindle must be at right angles to the disc for the top to spin properly

In contrast to the camera, the human eye with its constant gaze sees the colours merge into white

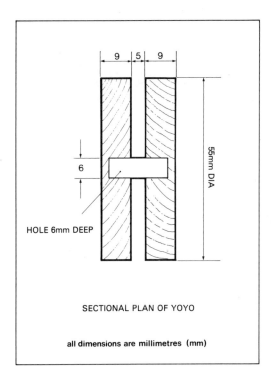

SECTIONAL PLAN OF YOYO

all dimensions are millimetres (mm)

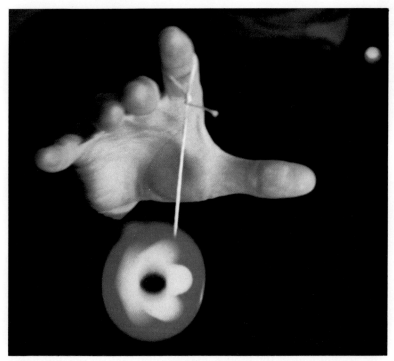

Yoyo

Materials required

1 piece of 9 mm plywood 120 × 60 mm
20 mm length of 6-mm diameter dowel rod
750 mm length of nylon twine

This type of yoyo is a traditional one, made from two round pieces of painted plywood plus an axle. Each main piece has a diameter of 55 mm and is 9 mm thick, and they must be of equal weight. This means that both must be cut and finished in exactly the same way.

The inside face should be very smooth, otherwise this would upset the up and down movement of the yoyo caused by centrifugal force. To make this up and down movement possible, there must be a central axle between the two parts 6 mm in diameter and 17 mm in length. Each end of the axle is fitted into a hole drilled at the exact centre of each of the parts. The correct position of this hole is vital for the movement of the yoyo. It should be 6 mm deep. Thus the two parts should be 5 mm apart when the axle is fitted. It is essential that they are absolutely parallel.

To attach the string, a small groove, equal to the depth of the hole, is made at one end of the axle. A piece of strong, fine string 750 mm long is then wound round the axle. It is best to use synthetic fibre for the string since it will not be affected by humidity. Only the two round parts are painted, using non-lead-containing paints.

Village

Materials required

1 square of 12 mm plywood 300 × 300 mm
1 piece of pine (or deal) 18 × 18 × 60 mm
1 piece of triangular-section pine (or deal) moulding
24 × 24 × 24 mm

In making this miniature village, the choice of colours and designs
is left to your imagination and flair. As the various components
are easy to make, you should be able to build this little village at
very low cost, with only a few mouldings and thin pieces of wood.

Small flat pieces can be cut out of 12 mm plywood. First, you
should draw the exact designs of each of the parts on the piece of
wood. If you have only a very narrow sheet, position your parts
in staggered rows so as not to waste any wood. Drawing
symmetrical elements is done by first drawing the left-hand side of
the design, then turning the tracing paper upside down to draw
the second half of the design, making sure that the second half is
positioned along the axis of symmetry. Use a fret-saw to cut out
the different parts. Depending on thickness, 2 to 6 sheets can be
clamped and cut simultaneously.

Scale 1:1

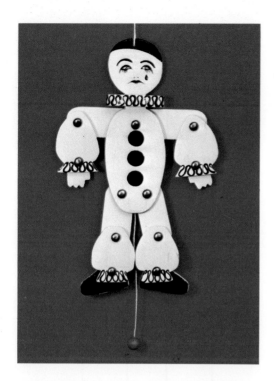

Pierrot doll

Materials required

1 piece of 6 mm plywood 225 × 200 mm
11 brass split-pins
1 metre of fine nylon twine

No selection of wooden toys would be complete without Pierrot, looking very realistic in his black and white painted costume. He is made of thirteen parts cut out from 6 mm plywood. The body and the head form a single part. They are separated by a small neck decorated with a semi-circular ruff. As the arms and legs are perfectly symmetrical, they can be drawn using the same template. The lower limbs are composed of a conventional thigh, leg and foot each, but the upper arms are made from a single piece of wood, thus exaggerating the jerky, loose-limbed movements typical of pantomime characters like Pierrot. The different parts are joined together using rivets, screws, split-pins or draw-pins. Great care should be taken when making the holes,' which preferably should be made with a small hand drill. Before positioning the strings, make sure that all parts move freely around their pivot and do not affect each other's movement. File any parts which rub against each other.

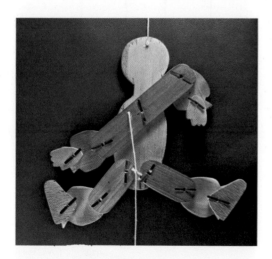

Split pin used to hold the parts together

Scale 2:3

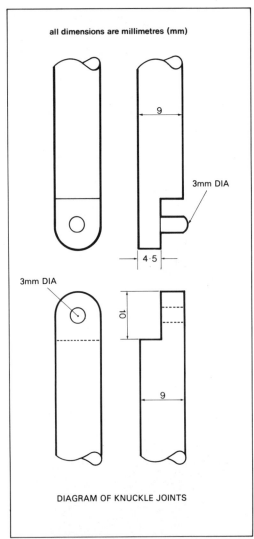

all dimensions are millimetres (mm)

3mm DIA

4·5

3mm DIA

DIAGRAM OF KNUCKLE JOINTS

Wooden puppets

Materials required

1 piece of 6 mm plywood 130 × 90 mm
1 piece of 3 mm plywood 120 × 60 mm
1 piece of 1 mm plastic laminate 100 × 12 mm
550 mm length of 12-mm diameter dowel rod
8 wooden beads, 18 mm diameter
4 wooden beads, 24 mm diameter
225 mm length of 3-mm diameter dowel rod
4 nuts and bolts, 2 mm diameter and 35 mm long
20 mm length of 24-mm diameter dowel rod
Small quantity of cotton wool
Model-size tins of enamels, various colours

On these two pages, we show you how to make two wooden puppets – an ambitious project but a very attractive one. Although these two characters look complicated, they are easy to build if you simply follow the instructions given below. Three types of component are used: plywood (for the body and the hands), dowel (for the arms and legs) and beads (for the head and some joints).

The man

The body is made from two sheets of plywood 6 mm thick with rounded edges (dimensions: 35 × 5 mm). These two pieces are drilled and countersunk as shown in the picture. N.B: To ensure

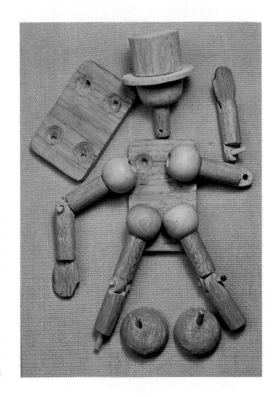

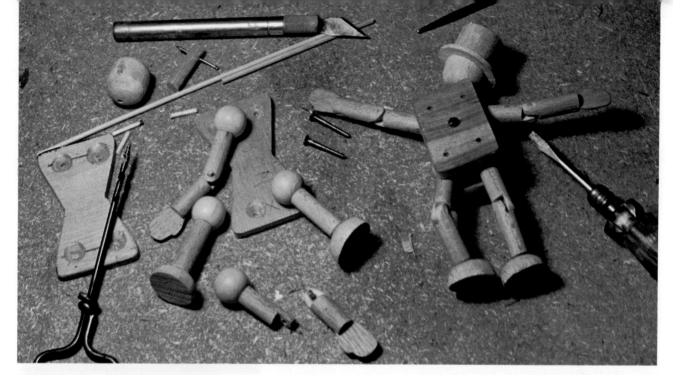

that the holes are in exactly the same place in each board, they must be drilled at the same time, held in position together. The distance between the holes (centre to centre) is 22 mm widthwise and 31 mm lengthwise. They are assembled with a nut and a bolt, holding the four beads for the joints in four circular housings. Both boards are also drilled at the top in order to attach a small piece of dowel forming the neck. The head can be made out of a half bead (24 mm). It is attached to the body by a piece of dowel.

Since both characters are made on a small scale, the dowels are particularly thin (3 mm), and matchsticks are ideal substitutes. This technique has also been adopted elsewhere for other constructions.

The hat is made from two parts glued together: a disc (diameter 50 mm) cut out of a sheet 3 mm thick, and a cylinder 18 mm high with a diameter of 24 mm. The hat is then glued onto the flat top of the head.

For the arms we have used a beech dowel (diameter 12 mm). A halving joint is used for the elbow and the knee. Both parts of the legs and the arms are 30 mm long and pivot around a 3-mm dowel. The hand, cut from a sheet of plastic laminate 1 mm thick, is fitted into a slot at the end of the forearm. The arm is hinged to the body with a bead rotating inside the countersunk holes drilled on both sheets. The bead is joined to the arm by a glued dowel. The legs are made in the same way. The only difference is that the lower part is attached to a half bead forming the foot, joined by a glued dowel.

The woman

This character is of similar construction, but with some variations. The legs are made up of a single section instead of two. They are joined in a similar way but the two parts of the body are larger to form the shape of the dress. The head is different, too. It is completely round.

Before being joined together, the two main parts are painted with non-lead-content paint.

The front and back can also be held together with a round-headed wood screw

Joining the head to the body with a lost-head nail

Rattle

Materials required

1 piece of beech 135 × 45 × 18 mm
1 piece of beech 105 × 25 × 3 mm
1 piece of beech 70 × 70 × 9 mm
200 mm length of 18-mm diameter dowel rod
75 mm length of 9-mm diameter dowel rod
1 × 25-mm no. 4 wood screw (countersunk head)
2 × 12-mm no. 6 wood screws (round head)
Small quantity of resin 'W' glue

Fixing the toothed wheel

The rattle shown here is one of the simplest to make. It is made of five parts, two of them being cylindrical.

The noise is produced by the end of a small thin blade of wood striking a toothed wheel when the rattle is swung. For a louder sound, it is best not to paint the rattle. The toothed wheel must be made of a suitable hardwood – preferably beech – otherwise the teeth will split off where the grain is short.

The interval between the teeth determines the frequency of the sunds. A wheel with fewer than six teeth will produce a staccato noise, whereas a wheel with more than six teeth will produce a more continuous and even one. You can cut as many teeth as you wish, provided you have regard to the length of the small blade and the intervals between the teeth, as well as to the outer diameter of the wheel in relation to the size of the slot.

The central hole has a diameter of 8 mm. The wheel (8 mm thick) is screwed onto the axle, using a 25-mm no. 4 screw. The axle (70 mm long) is fitted into the handle (197 mm long with a diameter of 18 mm). The flexible blade is 2.5 mm thick and 103 mm long. It is glued and screwed to the heaviest part of the rattle, which provides the momentum.

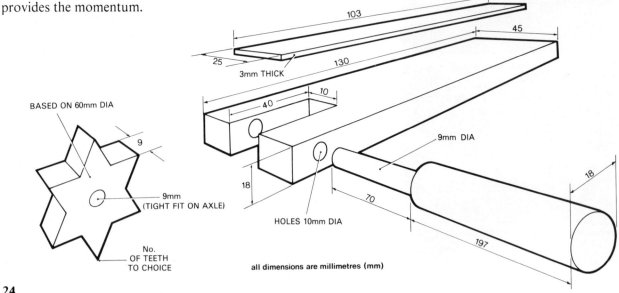

BASED ON 60mm DIA

9

9mm (TIGHT FIT ON AXLE)

No. OF TEETH TO CHOICE

103

45

25

130

3mm THICK

10

40

18

70

9mm DIA

18

HOLES 10mm DIA

197

all dimensions are millimetres (mm)

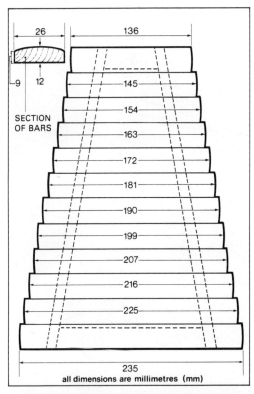

SECTION
OF BARS

26 · 136 · 9 · 12 · 145 · 154 · 163 · 172 · 181 · 190 · 199 · 207 · 216 · 225 · 235

all dimensions are millimetres (mm)

Rubber strips to cut out unwanted vibration

Bevelling the bars

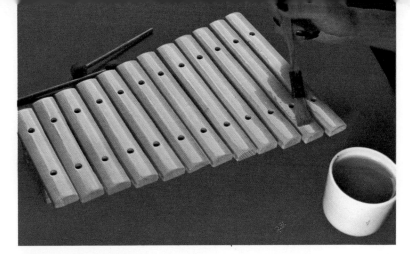

Xylophone

Materials required

2 × 1.25-m lengths of ash 30 × 12 mm in section
700 mm length of pine (or deal) 24 × 12 mm in section
200 mm length of pine (or deal) 24 × 6 mm in section
135 mm length of 6-mm diameter dowel rod
1 wooden bead, 24 mm diameter
700 mm length of thin rubber, 10 mm wide
24 × 25-mm flat-headed round nails
Small quantity of polyurethane (clear) varnish

The xylophone is made up of 12 ash bars, representing 12 different notes, spanning more than one octave. Each bar is 26 mm wide at its base and 9 mm thick at each side. The upper face of each bar is rounded, not flat (see diagram). The thickness of the bar in the middle is 12 mm. All the bars should have the same dimensions, the only difference being their length. From the longest to the smallest, the lengths are: 235 – 225 – 216 – 207 – 199 – 190 – 181 – 172 – 163 – 154 – 145 – 136 mm. They are spaced about 3 mm apart and each bar is drilled at either end, each hole being 9 mm deep with a diameter of 7 mm. The holes are situated at the following distances from the end of each bar, again going from the longest bar to the smallest: 46.5 – 45.5 – 43.5 – 41.5 – 40 – 38.5 – 38 – 37 – 35 – 33.5 – 32 mm. To obtain the correct range of sounds, you will have to bevel the lower part of 5 of the 12 bars. Using a bevel gauge, the 190 mm bar should be bevelled at 13° for 20 mm, the 154 mm and 145 mm bars at 18° for 23 mm. The 181 mm bar should be bevelled at both ends, one at 18° for 21 mm and the other one at 18° for 4 mm. Every modification should be perpendicular to the central axis of the xylophone, which is equal to its total length (340 mm).

The base is made up of two long pieces (340 × 12 × 24 mm) and two cross-pieces (150 × 24 × 6 mm; 74 × 24 × 6 mm) which are joined by an open mortise and tenon joint.

The two cross-pieces are positioned in slots made halfway along. The bars are placed on two narrow rubber strips glued to the two long pieces. They are held firmly in position by flat-headed nails 25 mm long, driven into circular holes.

The hammer is made from a stick 130 mm long and 6 mm in diameter, inserted into a small wooden bead (diameter 24 mm).

The last stage is the varnishing of the upper part and the sides of the bars.

Cicada

Materials required

1 piece of 3 mm plywood 250 × 150 mm
25 mm length of 6-mm diameter dowel rod
1 wooden ball, approximately 24 mm diameter
2 coloured beads, approximately 6 mm diameter
Model-size tins of enamels, various colours

This little toy is made of eight parts. Two of them are cut out of a piece of dowel 6 mm in diameter. Each is 11 mm long, equal to the thickness of the three pieces they join together. They act as pivots for the two inner and two outer wings. The wings and the body are cut out of a sheet of plywood 3 mm thick. For the head you can either use a small block of wood or a small bead. It should be 24 mm in diameter for a wingspan of 80 mm. You can choose whichever scale you want provided you respect the proportions of the design. The body, cut out of the same sheet as the wings, is slotted into the head. The eyes are made from beads about 6 mm in diameter. Then the cicada can be either painted or stained as you wish.

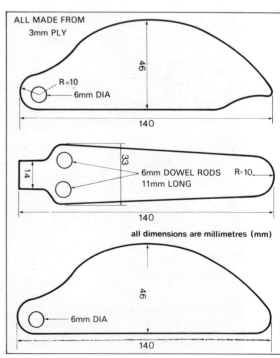

ALL MADE FROM
3mm PLY

46

R=10
6mm DIA

140

14   33
6mm DOWEL RODS   R=10
11mm LONG

140

all dimensions are millimetres (mm)

46

6mm DIA

140

Cut-out animals

Ensuring that the dowels are square when gluing; a try-square can equally well be used

Materials required

1 piece 6 mm plywood 300 × 90 mm
200 mm length of 6-mm diameter dowel rod
Model-size tins of enamels, various colours

More 6 mm plywood if further cut-out animals are to be made

This modular toy is of great interest to children. Indeed, its undoubted educational value makes it a very good toy. It is made using standard shapes (we have chosen two well-known animals: the horse and the giraffe). Of course, many other motifs could equally be chosen, preferably motifs which can be identified by children in order to contribute to the development of their manipulative abilities. The animals can be cut out of sheets 6 mm thick. It is essential that all the holes should be bored at the same time, holding all the parts together with clamps. The drill must be held vertically in order to be able to thread each animal onto the dowel.

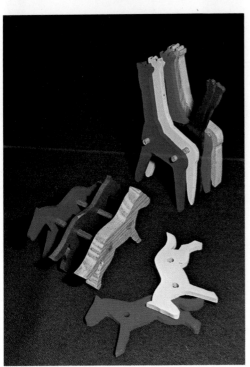

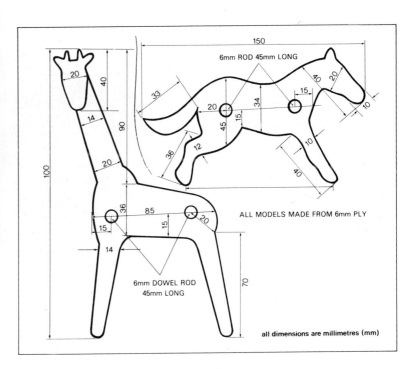

Stilts

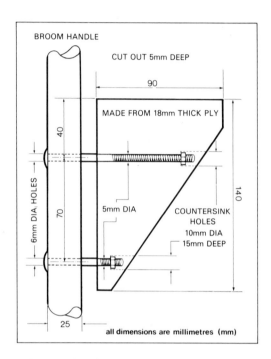

BROOM HANDLE
CUT OUT 5mm DEEP
90
MADE FROM 18mm THICK PLY
40
6mm DIA. HOLES
70
5mm DIA
140
COUNTERSINK HOLES
10mm DIA
15mm DEEP
25
all dimensions are millimetres (mm)

Gluing the bolts and the surfaces in contact strengthens the joint

To get off to a good start, try leaning against a wall

Materials required

2 sturdy (and straight) wooden broom handles
1 piece of 18 mm plywood 300 × 100 mm
2 × 125-mm bolts, 5 mm diameter
2 × 50-mm bolts, 5 mm diameter
2 rubber ferrules to fit lower ends of broom handles
Small quantity of clear varnish

You could hardly find anything easier to make than a pair of stilts. With these tall wooden legs a child can rise well above the ground to look far beyond his usual horizon. These wooden legs are an outlet for imagination and also a great advantage for walking over muddy ground (but warn children that they must not venture into any real quagmires).

Good balance, essential for walking on stilts, is linked to forward motion, which enables the stilt-walker to keep control. (We cannot accept responsibility for those who want to remain motionless on their stilts.) This is why we recommend practice before starting out; bold steps are better than hesitant ones.

Each wooden upright is about 1.5 m high with a diameter of 23 mm (a broom handle is ideal); the triangular foot-rests in plywood (thickness: 18 mm) are 100 mm long and are positioned in a notch cut 3 mm deep 300 mm from the foot of the upright. They are secured by two long, thin bolts countersunk at the wider end of each foot-rest.

Cinema

Materials required

1 piece of 6 mm plywood 500 × 410 mm
1 piece of pine (or deal) 310 × 70 × 30 mm
1 piece of pine (or deal) 310 × 70 × 12 mm
400 mm length of 18-mm diameter dowel rod
25 mm length of 24-mm diameter dowel rod
100 mm length of 6-mm diameter dowel rod
30 mm length of 30-mm diameter dowel rod
1 piece of beech (or other suitable hardwood) 100 × 20 × 6 mm
1 piece of beech or ash 40 × 8 × 1 mm
1 piece of beech 75 × 6 × 6 mm
1 piece of cartridge paper 200 × 200 mm
2 fibre washers 25-mm diameter with centre hole of approximately 9-mm diameter
1 25-mm panel-pin
Small quantity of resin 'W' glue
Quantity of polyurethane (clear) varnish

It is not difficult to make this little 'cartoon cinema'. If you follow the instructions carefully you should have the pleasure of seeing it work realistically, i.e. you should be able to recreate the movement of the little character drawn 16 times on the front face of the disc.

All the parts should be cut out with great precision and should be carefully finished, in particular the small parts and the toothed wheel. The panels of the main box, the disc, and the toothed wheel are cut out of 6 mm plywood. The pillars are in beech, the base and the top in pine. Because of their mechanical functions, the axle, the handle, and the wedge of the blade are cut out of beech or any other suitable hardwood.

The disc has an inner diameter of 194 mm with a square hole in its centre. The toothed wheel has an outer diameter of 166 mm and an inner diameter of 134 mm. Each of the 16 teeth is 8 mm wide at the base and 5 mm wide at the top. The wheel also has a square hole and is glued onto the disc. This operation should preferably be done at the end, once the drawings have been copied on and the blade has been fixed to the wedge, so that the drawings are correctly positioned in the window.

Shaping and gluing the parts

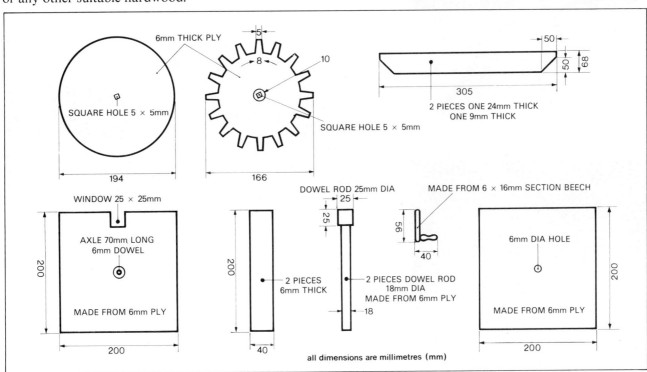

6mm THICK PLY

SQUARE HOLE 5 × 5mm

194

166

SQUARE HOLE 5 × 5mm

50

305

68

50

2 PIECES ONE 24mm THICK
ONE 9mm THICK

WINDOW 25 × 25mm

AXLE 70mm LONG
6mm DOWEL

200

200

MADE FROM 6mm PLY

200

40

2 PIECES
6mm THICK

DOWEL ROD 25mm DIA

25

25

200

2 PIECES DOWEL ROD
18mm DIA
MADE FROM 6mm PLY

18

MADE FROM 6 × 16mm SECTION BEECH

56

40

6mm DIA HOLE

200

200

MADE FROM 6mm PLY

all dimensions are millimetres (mm)

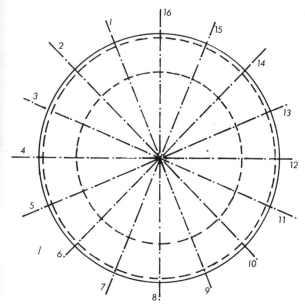

2

1. *Arrangement of the drawings on the disc 2. Breakdown of the movement into 16 images to give a complete cycle. Any further cartoons you make should also consists of 16 images 3. Blade for slowing down the movement; it should be as stiff as possible 4. Fitting the handle to the crank*

3

4

The axle is 70 mm long. The crank (56 mm long × 16 mm wide × 6 mm thick) is fitted to the axle through a square hole (6 × 6 mm). The dowel of the handle (40 × 16 × 6 mm) is inserted into the circular hole drilled at one end of the crank.

To make it easier, start by gluing the front panel. A window (200 × 200 × 6 mm) has been cut out of the front panel. Then glue the two side panels (40 × 200 × 6 mm) to the pine base and top, making sure the box is well centred. These two parts in pine are the same shape and are cut out of a 68 × 305 mm block, the base being 26 mm thick and the top 10 mm thick. Note that a 50 × 20 × 52 mm right-angled triangle of wood is cut away from the front corners. The pillars (diameter 18 mm) are also glued to the top and the base. The blade (1 mm thick; 7 mm wide) is fitted and glued to the corner wedge (14 × 8 × 4 × 7 × 7 × 4 mm). The blade is square at the end and its length depends upon the nature and the flexibility of the wood chosen.

The characters can be drawn either with ink or by pokerwork. They must be evenly spaced. After decoration you can varnish the toy.

But the cinema will not work unless you add a small circular stop 17 mm high with a hole in its centre (diameter 10 mm). This stop should be threaded onto the axle to prevent the disc from slipping. You should also add two fibre washers to be threaded onto the axle, four small wedges to hold the back panel to the two sides, and a small draw-pin on the axle at the back of the box to hold everything in position. The first washer is placed between the disc and the front panel, while the second one is placed between the front panel and the crank.

Assembly

Pokerwork decoration

Making the four holes in the fish's body for attaching the fins and suspending the mobile

Attaching the fins to the body with nylon thread

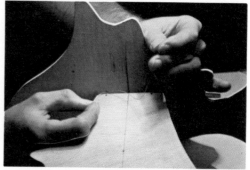

Mobile

Materials required
1 piece of 6 mm plywood 450 × 200 mm
3 metres of nylon thread
Model-size tins of enamels, various colours

Decorating with coloured adhesive film

The important thing with this model is to make sure that all the suspension points balance perfectly. The cutting of the different parts is a very easy job. The thickness of the central body does not matter too much (although it should still be of a reasonable size, say 6 mm), but both fins must be of equal weight. They should be cut from the same sheet and have the same shape. The fins meet the body slightly below the centre of gravity to enable the body to remain in a vertical position. Balancing the model varies according to the shape of the design. To find the centre of gravity of each part, balance it on a ruler. The points where the two threads are attached to the fish should be situated on a straight line passing through the centres of gravity of the fins and the body (the measures are taken when the parts are symmetrically positioned). The space between the two points of suspension is determined by moving along the line (use adhesive tape for this) until the fins are inclined slightly downwards. The fins are tied together with a nylon thread passed through the four holes drilled in the body where the fins meet it.

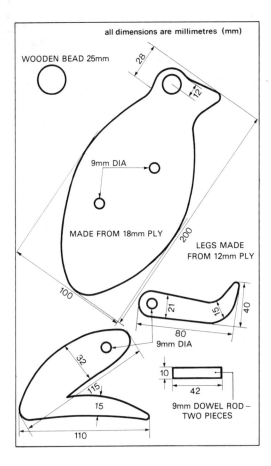

all dimensions are millimetres (mm)

WOODEN BEAD 25mm

28

12

9mm DIA

MADE FROM 18mm PLY

200

100

LEGS MADE
FROM 12mm PLY

21

15

40

80

9mm DIA

32

115

15

110

10

42

9mm DOWEL ROD –
TWO PIECES

Frog

Materials required

1 piece of 18 mm plywood 210 × 105 mm
1 piece of 12 mm plywood 550 × 150 mm
100 mm length of 9-mm diameter dowel rod
1 wooden bead, 25-mm diameter
Coloured vinyl sheets OR model-size tins of enamels, various colours
Small quantity of adhesive

Although this charming little frog does not enjoy the same agility as his flesh-and-blood fellows, his physical qualities, such as toughness and life-expectancy, are very impressive. And what's more, he can be easily tamed. As well as his robustness and size, the frog has other attributes: for example, his hind legs can rotate through 210°! All these qualities combine to make this an exceptional frog indeed.

The body is cut out of a sheet of multi-ply (7 ply) 18 mm thick and 200 mm long. The four legs are cut from 12 mm thick multi-ply (5 ply). They are joined to the body by a wooden axle 9 mm in diameter. The eyes are made from two half beads 25 mm in diameter.

There are few ways of decorating pine. Here, as with the mobile, small shapes have been cut out from adhesive film. This has the advantage of not marking the wood: paint and stains tend to spread over the open grain of softwoods

Dogs

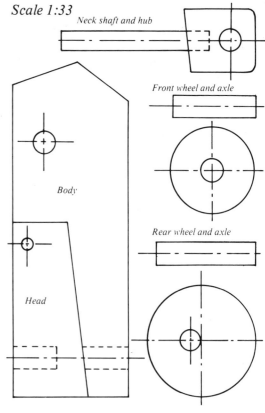

Scale 1:33

Neck shaft and hub

Front wheel and axle

Body

Rear wheel and axle

Head

These two little dogs have a most unusual pedigree: they are probably the only dogs you have seen which were conceived by man but are descended from pine! We bet you won't have any trouble getting along with them and that you'll give them all the care and attention they deserve.

They are just one example of toys on wheels. But these are wheels with a difference. Because the rear axle is off-centre, the dogs waggle as the distance between the axle and the ground (the vertical radius) constantly changes.

The dogs are made up of the following components: the body, made of a 50-mm thick piece (larger dog) and a 40-mm thick piece (smaller dog); the head, cut out of the same piece as the body in the case of the larger dog, and from 24 mm plywood for the smaller dog; two front and two rear wheels (12 mm multi-ply); three axles (18 mm diameter); two pieces of thin (3 mm) leather for the ears; a 35 mm hub; and a small piece of leather for the tail. If the dog is to be pulled along, you will also need to attach a stout length of string to the dog's 'chest' with an eyelet screw or staple. These two toys can be made to any scale, as indeed can most of the others in this book.

Materials required

1 piece of pine (or deal) 550 × 50 × 50 mm
1 piece of pine (or deal) 200 × 40 × 40 mm
1 piece of 24 mm plywood 100 × 50 mm
1 piece of 12 mm plywood 300 × 200 mm
150 mm length of 18-mm diameter dowel rod
350 mm length of 12-mm diameter dowel rod
Small quantity of leather for the ears and tails
Small quantity of resin 'W' glue

Materials required

1 piece of 12 mm plywood 500 × 90 mm
1 piece of 6 mm plywood 150 × 125 mm
200 mm length of 9-mm diameter dowel rod
1 piece of canvas, dimensions to suit choice of tail
Rectangles of wood forming tail can be cut from the waste from the plywood
2 wooden beads, 12 mm diameter
100 mm length of 6-mm diameter dowel rod
Small quantity of resin 'W' glue
Small quantity of enamel to chosen colour

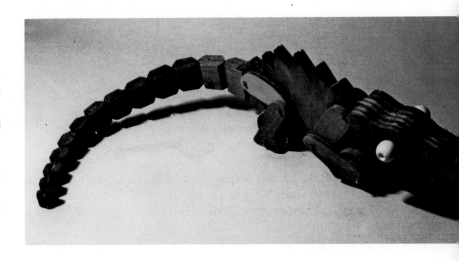

Iguana

The stability of this little iguana depends on the thickness of its four wheels. The axles have a diameter of 9 mm, the same as the two pieces of dowel which join the legs to the body. For the other joints you can use either rivets or dowel. The iguana's legs are 6 mm thick and are each made of two parts.

The quality of the finished toy will depend on the accuracy of your cutting. The drilling of the holes and the fitting of the axles must be done with great care. The distance between the axles must be exactly equal at either side or else the toy will not roll properly. Note that the length of the axles should be slightly greater than the total thickness of the pieces of wood they pass through (allow 2 to 3 mm play).

The iguana's body can be made of 12 mm multi-ply. The head and body are made of a single piece, and the head is formed by sticking two additional pieces to either side. The tail is made by sticking small, bevelled rectangles of wood to both sides of a long strip of stout canvas. This allows the component parts of the tail to pivot slightly on a vertical plane and it will move from side to side.

Constructing the tail

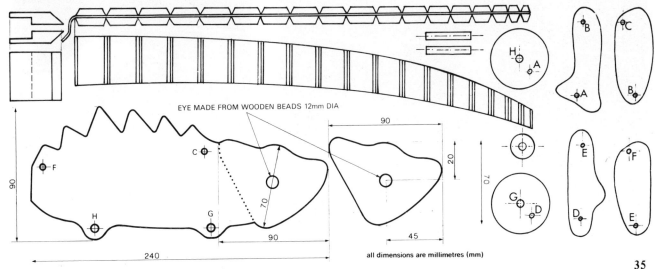

EYE MADE FROM WOODEN BEADS 12mm DIA

all dimensions are millimetres (mm)

Alpine chalet

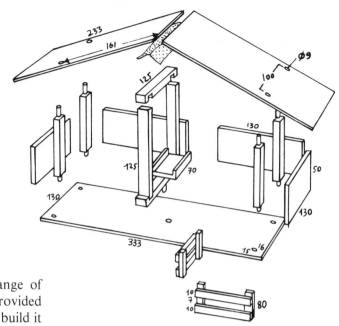

Materials required

1 piece of 6 mm plywood 530 × 320 mm
1 piece of pine (or deal) 900 × 12 × 8 mm
6 × 1-m lengths of 6-mm diameter dowel rod
Troughs may be made from the 6 mm plywood waste
1 piece of canvas 130 × 40 mm
1 piece of 12 mm plywood 300 × 300 mm for 10 animals
Small quantity of resin 'W' glue
Model-size tins of enamels, various colours

This small Alpine chalet can be made from a wide range of woods. In some cases you can combine different woods. Provided you keep to the relative proportions you are even free to build it on whatever scale you wish.

It is preferable to use solid wood for the pillars and the central support. These are cut from an 85 mm length of 10 × 7 mm wood. For the roof and the base we have used 6 mm plywood, thick enough not to warp after gluing. The walls are cut out of the same sheet (total size: 45 × 35 mm). The 'log cabin' effect is achieved by gluing pieces of dowel 6 mm in diameter horizontally on to the walls (see photographs). Use mortise joints to assemble the four pieces which constitute the central support.

The roof is made of two identical parts which are hinged by gluing to a 130 mm strip of cloth. The roof is not glued on: it is simply placed on the four corner pillars and held in position by four pieces of dowel which slot into holes made in the roof. The two small troughs are carved out of 6 mm plywood.

The animals have been cut from wood 12 mm thick; the proportionate distance between the front and hind legs, in the case of the cow, is 28 mm. If the wood used is thicker or thinner, then the distance between front and hind legs will be greater or smaller proportionately.

Penny-farthing (see cover)

Materials required

1 piece of 9 mm plywood 320 × 125 mm
1 piece of 6 mm plywood 270 × 240 mm
1-metre length of 9-mm diameter dowel rod
1-metre length of 18-mm diameter dowel rod for the pusher stick
10 fibre washers to fit tightly onto the 9-mm diameter dowel rod
2 × 18-mm panel-pins
Small quantity of resin 'W' glue
Model-size tins of enamels, various colours

Like any other articulated toy, this penny-farthing will not work properly unless all the parts, and especially the wheels, the hubs, the pedals and the legs, are traced and cut out very accurately. Remember that the distances between the joints of the moving parts must be exactly the same, otherwise the foot will not rotate around the hub but will stick. The moving parts here are the thigh and the lower leg, which are jointed at the hip, the knee and the foot. We stress yet again that these important holes must be drilled as straight as possible. This is essential if the dowels are to rotate smoothly in their housings.

All the flat parts are made from 6 mm plywood, except for the central part (9 mm). The parts can be painted using oil paints. In theory no preparation is needed. But if the surface is not smooth you can sand the parts with glasspaper and then undercoat them. To avoid warping, paint each part on both sides.

The parts are assembled using 9 mm beech dowel, except where the handle is joined to the central piece and the handle-bars are joined to the hands. Some dowels are glued in place, but seven are not: the pivot for the shoulders, the pivot for the hips, the pivots for the knees (on the inside), the hub of the large wheel, and the pivots for the pedals. Note that the hubs are themselves made of dowel.

Making the notch (a through mortise would be a stronger alternative) for attaching the handle-bars to the forks

Those dowels which are not glued must be able to turn freely. The diameters of the holes for these, including the holes in the forks, are enlarged to let the joints move smoothly. To prevent the parts from slipping out of position, fix them with a draw-pin on the

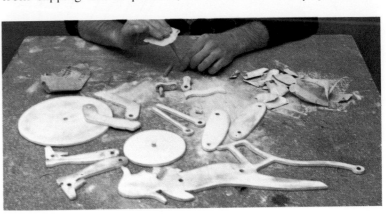

For a smoother finish, sand all the parts with glasspaper

inside and with a washer glued on the outside. The washer should be driven on to the slightly tapered end of the dowel. An alternative, stronger, method of fixing the dowels is shown in the diagram. There are nine joints of this kind: the mounting of the rear wheel on its hub, where the feet are joined to the pedals, at the knees (on the inside), at the hips and the front axle in the forks.

The two hands are simply glued to the handle-bars once these have been notched and glued to the frame. The forks are likewise glued and pinned to the frame.

To cut out the piece from the centre of the frame, first make a hole for the fretsaw blade in the area which is to be removed. With this type of model it is best to drill all the holes before cutting out the parts, especially small parts such as the pedals.

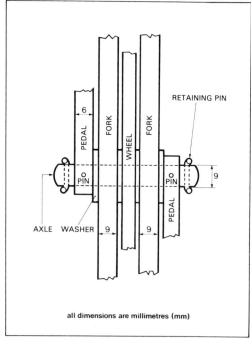

Fixing the axle-pins

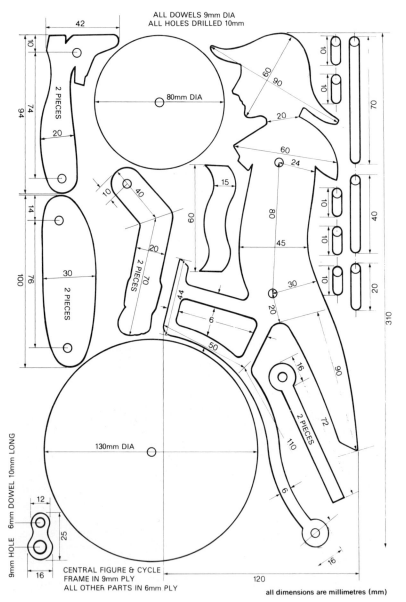

Spray-painting the components

Pink flamingo

Materials required

1 piece of 6 mm plywood 130 × 110 mm
1 piece of 3 mm plywood 85 × 30 mm
350 mm length of 3-mm diameter nylon cord
600 mm length of 10-mm diameter bamboo cane
3 metres of very fine nylon thread
Small quantity of resin 'W' glue
Model-size tins of enamels, various colours

This pink flamingo is suspended from a frame like a puppet on a string and can be made to move just like a real puppet.

It is made of only six pieces of plywood. The head, body and feet are cut out of a 6 mm sheet. The wings, however, are cut out of 3 mm plywood and are then glued to the body. The parts are connected by nylon cord. You need 150 mm for the neck and 100 mm for each leg. (Singe the end to stop the cord unravelling.) Drill holes 9 mm deep of the same diameter as the cord (3 mm) in the wood to receive the glued ends of the lengths of cord.

The frame is a small bamboo cross, to the ends of which are attached the four nylon threads (you will need 2 to 3 metres of thread in all). They vary in length according to which part of the model they support. Adjust the suspension points so that the model is at right angles to the frame and the threads are straight.

Making thread holes in the bamboo frame

Scale 1:1

Self-propelled figure

Materials required

1 piece of 9 mm plywood 600 × 60 mm
160 mm length of 6-mm diameter dowel rod
Small quantity of resin 'W' glue
Model-size tins of white, red, brown, pink, and green enamels

This model is in a class of its own. As you can see, the figure moves under the force of gravity. Made of a single piece, it is placed at the top of the slide and under its own weight tumbles to the bottom between the pegs. It is made of 9 mm plywood and decorated with enamel paints. Five colours have been used: white, red, brown, pink and green.

The pegs which catch the figure on its way down the slide are 6 mm in diameter. They must be correctly placed if the toy is to work. Therefore we advise you to space the pegs exactly as shown on the diagram. The angle of the slide is varied by hand.

The base and the slide are made of plywood, though many other kinds of wood would be equally suitable.

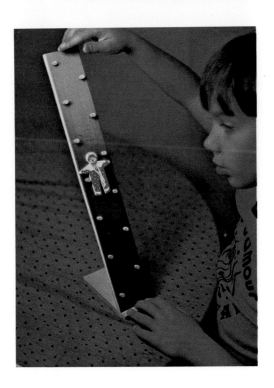

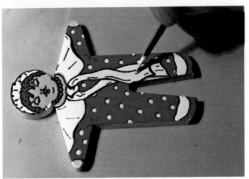

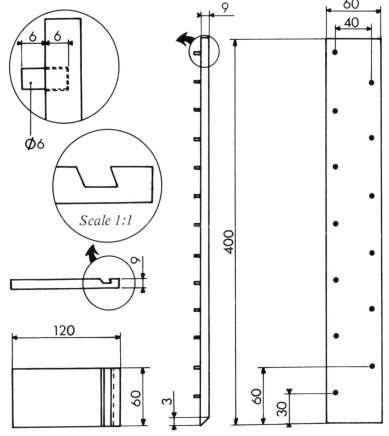

Scale 1:1

Rocking-horse

Materials required

1 piece of 18 mm plywood 1.10 × 1.00 m
2 × 1-metre lengths of 25-mm diameter dowel rod
1-metre length of 9-mm diameter dowel rod
Quantity of coarse wool for mane
1 staple to secure mane to head
¼ litre of all-weather marine varnish

This rocking-horse is one of a series of collapsible toys which are held together by draw-pins. The parts are cut out of 18 mm pine multi-ply, which makes the model very strong. Use a sheet of 5-ply measuring 1.10 × 1.00 m. Follow the plan below in order to economise on wood and to simplify the tracing of the outlines. The grain and any knots can enhance the horse's appearance, so use your skill to place them in your cutting plan where they will be most striking – at the eyes, for example.

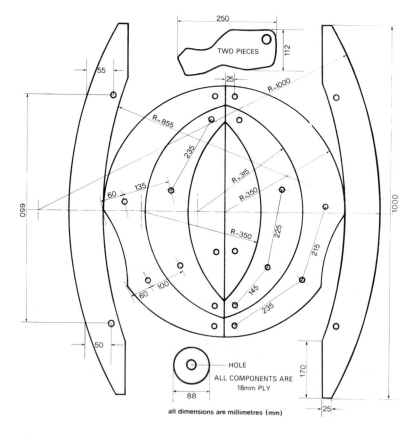

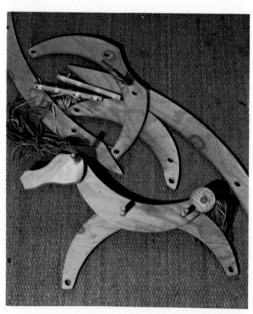

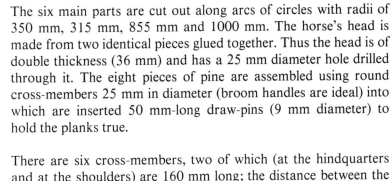

The six main parts are cut out along arcs of circles with radii of 350 mm, 315 mm, 855 mm and 1000 mm. The horse's head is made from two identical pieces glued together. Thus the head is of double thickness (36 mm) and has a 25 mm diameter hole drilled through it. The eight pieces of pine are assembled using round cross-members 25 mm in diameter (broom handles are ideal) into which are inserted 50 mm-long draw-pins (9 mm diameter) to hold the planks true.

There are six cross-members, two of which (at the hindquarters and at the shoulders) are 160 mm long; the distance between the axes of the draw-pins is 120 mm. This distance on the tail cross-member is 76 mm (120 mm long). Make sure you drill the draw-pin holes slightly closer together than the total thickness of the horse. You will have to use a clamp to assemble it. The two cross-members at the feet are 330 mm long, and draw-pin holes are drilled at 41, 64, 116, 188, 211, 263 and 286 mm. The cross-member holding the head in place sticks out on either side to form handles which the young rider can grip (25 mm in diameter and 30 mm long).

The mane and the tail can be made of wool or hemp knotted around a staple.

For safety, it is important that the ends of the draw-pins should be rounded.

Gymnast

Materials required

1 piece of 6 mm plywood 160 × 150 mm
1 piece of beech 400 × 10 × 5 mm
450 mm length of 12-mm diameter dowel rod
90 mm length of 6-mm diameter dowel rod
1 piece of 12 mm plywood 200 × 80 mm
Small quantity of resin 'W' glue
Model-size tins of enamels, various colours

Although the way this toy works is fairly simple, you must be very accurate in cutting out the figure from a piece of 6 mm-thick plywood. You must respect the relative dimensions of the parallel bars and the small cross-piece, both made of beech, and of the base (12 mm plywood) into which the four uprights are fitted. Do not paint either the bar or the cross-piece.

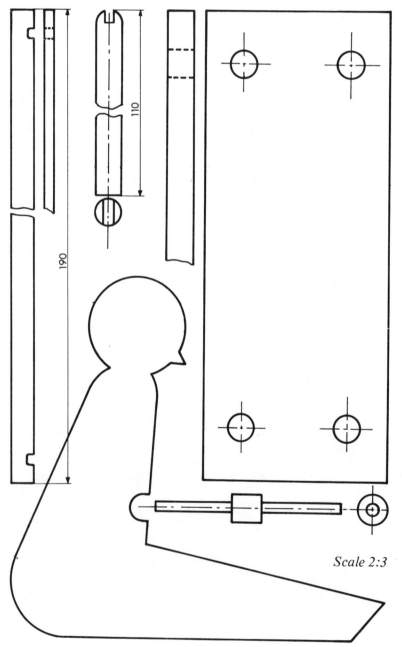

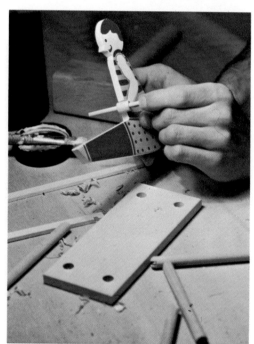

Gluing the cross-piece to the body

Scale 2:3

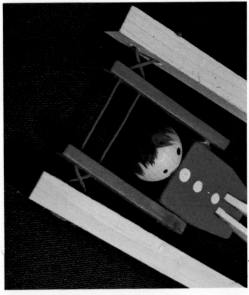

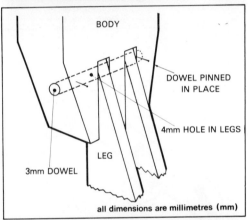

BODY

DOWEL PINNED
IN PLACE

4mm HOLE IN LEGS

LEG

3mm DOWEL

all dimensions are millimetres (mm)

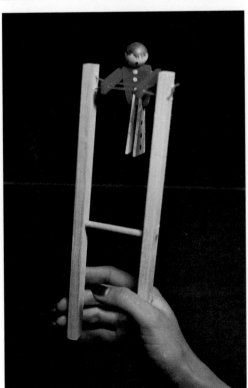

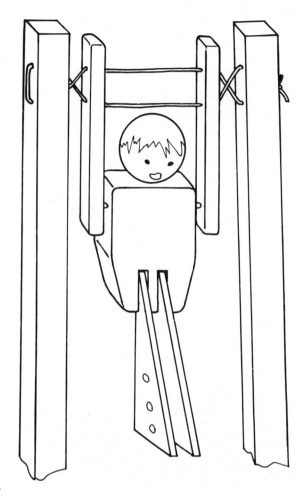

Acrobat

Materials required
1 piece of pine (or deal) 500 × 15 × 10 mm
85 mm length of 6-mm diameter dowel rod
100 mm length of 3-mm diameter dowel rod
1 wooden bead, 18 mm diameter
1 piece of 9 mm plywood 70 × 45 mm
1 piece of 3 mm plywood 100 × 30 mm
1 of piece of 6 mm plywood 110 × 9 mm
200 mm length of cord (not nylon)
1 × 6-mm panel-pin
Small quantity of resin 'W' glue
Model-size tins of enamels

This small toy is based on the principle of the tension of a cord
(180 mm long) divided into straight sections and crossing at two
points. The tension of the cord is produced by squeezing together
the lower ends of the uprights (230 × 9 × 15 mm). These pivot on
the small cross strut (71 mm × 6 mm diameter) placed 99 mm
from their bottom end. At rest, the gap between the two uprights
(to their outer edge) is 66 mm at the top and 74 mm at the
bottom. These distances are fixed once and for all on gluing.
The acrobat's joints are made with 3 mm diameter dowel. The
holes for the dowels are 4 mm in diameter to ensure free rotation.
Make the head from a 18 mm bead and fix it to the body with 6
mm diameter dowel. The body is 9 mm thick and has two notches
for the legs, which swing around a dowel. The thickness of the
arms is 6 mm and that of the legs 3 mm.

Cars

Materials required

1 piece of pine (or deal) 125 × 50 × 35 mm
300 mm length of 6-mm diameter dowel rod
1 piece of 1-mm plastic laminate 95 × 25 mm
1 piece of 9 mm plywood 40 × 20 mm
1 piece of 9 mm plywood 100 × 100 mm
50 mm length of 18-mm diameter dowel rod
50 mm length of 25-mm diameter dowel rod
1 piece of beech 80 × 40 × 36 mm
250 mm length of broom handle or 30-mm diameter dowel rod
1 piece of rubber tubing from which rings can be cut to stretch over 18-mm diameter dowel rod to simulate car tyres
4 × 25-mm metal staples, internal size 6 – 8 mm
1 × 25-mm no. 6 wood screw (round-headed)
1 piece of 6 mm plywood 300 × 30 mm
Small quantity of resin 'W' glue
Model-size tins of enamels, various colours

The three models described on these two pages are good illustrations of three woodwork techniques: using a block, using a cylindrical piece of wood, and using board.

Car with suspension

The main part of this car is made from a 122 × 50 × 35 mm block of pine with nine flat surfaces. Two surfaces constitute the parallel sides, both with the same profile, which means that all the other faces are at right angles to the sides. The bottom surface is 100 mm long, the bonnet 37 mm long, the radiator 19 mm, the roof 35 mm, and the back end 22 mm. Two wheel arches, 16 mm wide and about 5 mm deep are hollowed out of the bottom surface, 9 mm from the front and 6 mm from the rear, to give clearance to the wheels.

The U-shaped wheel guides are staples which are tapped into the wheel arches. The gap across the inside of the U is 6 mm. They are set 32 mm apart at both front and rear. The beech axles are 6 mm in diameter and 68 mm long, with a wheelbase of 67 mm. The laminated suspension board (1 × 95 × 24 mm) is screwed to a plywood rectangle (40 × 20 × 9 mm) in the centre of the underside of the block. The wheels, cut from beech dowel, are 18 mm in diameter and 10 mm thick. Each tyre is a rubber ring cut from a length of heavy-duty tubing. An overall diameter of 24 mm for wheel and tyre is required. Apply glue to the wooden wheels and push on the rubber tyres.

Racing car

The racing car is shaped from a piece of broom-handle 30 mm in diameter and 250 mm long. The rear wheels, shaped from a piece of beech, are 35 mm in diameter and 36 mm wide and are set 50 mm apart. The front wheels, which are 25 mm in diameter and 20 mm wide, are set 40 mm apart. The wheelbase is 130 mm. The·

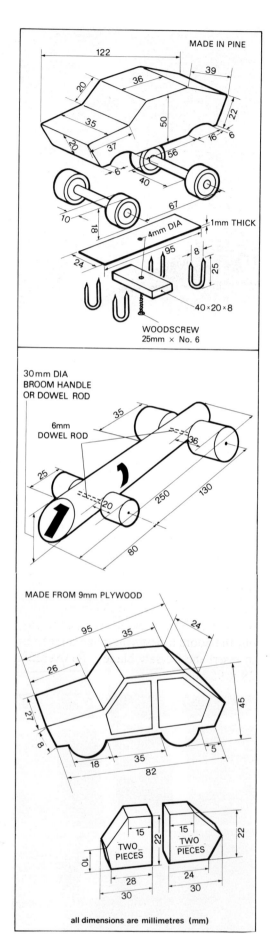

front axle is 9 mm above the underside of the car and the rear axle 15 mm. Holes are drilled 7 mm in diameter right through the body of the car to take the axles, which are 6 mm in diameter. The axles are glued on the ends and are pushed into the wheels and spin freely in the body.

Small car

This model is made entirely from 9 mm plywood. The main piece is made of three thicknesses glued together. It will be easier to cut out the doors if first you make a small hole in one corner in order to insert the fretsaw blade. The overall dimensions of the car are 28 × 95 mm.

Shaping and assembly: two important stages in the construction of these small vehicles

From left to right: car with suspension, undercoated, sanded and then varnished; racing car made from a broom-handle; small car made of plywood, the perfect educational toy

Aeroplane

Materials required

1 piece of pine (or deal) 180 × 35 × 25 mm
1 piece of 6 mm plywood 350 × 30 mm
140 mm length of 6-mm diameter dowel rod
40 mm length of 3-mm diameter dowel rod
1 piece of pine (or deal) 35 × 12 × 12 mm
25 mm length of broom handle or 30-mm diameter dowel rod
12 mm length of 18-mm diameter dowel rod
1 piece of pine (or deal) 70 × 9 × 9 mm
3 wooden beads, 12 mm diameter
1 wooden bead, 21 mm diameter
4 × 18-mm panel-pins
Small quantity of resin 'W' glue
Model-size tins of enamels, various colours

You will have fun making this small monoplane in natural and painted wood. It is of a very simple and logical design, well suited to working with wood. It reminds us that the first aeroplanes were made of wood and demonstrates the great skill and ingenuity used in their design.

We have chosen pine as the basic material, but many other woods could also be used. The central piece representing the fuselage is cut from a piece of wood 25 mm wide, 35 mm deep and 175 mm long. The nose is a 35 mm semi-circle of the same width as the fuselage at the front. The rear 100 mm of the fuselage tapers to a depth of 15 mm. The main wing is cut out of 6 mm plywood and has a span of 180 mm. The wing tips (at right angles to the trailing edge of the wing) are 29 mm wide and the two leading edges are each 91 mm long. The diagonal struts which join the wing to the fuselage are 66 mm long and 6 mm in diameter. Cut the rear wing from the same sheet as the front. It has a 93 mm span, 18 mm tips at right angles, and 48 mm leading edges. The tail, cut from the same sheet, is a trapezium measuring 25 × 25 × 15 × 27 mm.

The wheels (30 mm in diameter and 10 mm thick) are fitted to the ends of a rectangular block glued and screwed beneath the fuselage 100 mm from the tail. A 21 mm bead glued to the fuselage below the wing forms the pilot's head. The propeller, which is made of a cylinder (18 mm in diameter and 11 mm long) and two shaped pieces (35 mm long), spins on a 3 mm dowel which ends in a 12 mm diameter bead, as does the axle.

Lacing doll

Materials required

1 piece of 12 mm plywood 240 × 120 mm
Quantity of nylon cord

This American Indian doll is ideal for practising lacing. All sorts of stitches can be tried out. The wood is 12 mm thick and the diameter of the holes must not exceed 5 mm. Nylon cord is easier to thread than cord made from natural fibres.

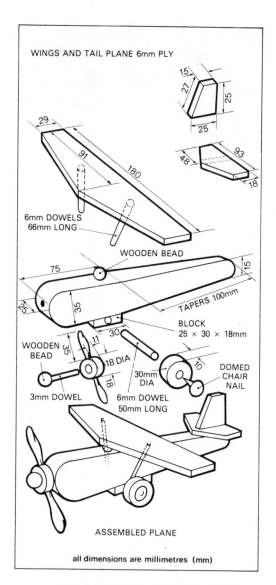

WINGS AND TAIL PLANE 6mm PLY

6mm DOWELS 66mm LONG

WOODEN BEAD

TAPERS 100mm

BLOCK 25 × 30 × 18mm

WOODEN BEAD

3mm DOWEL

18 DIA

6mm DOWEL 50mm LONG

30mm DIA

DOMED CHAIR NAIL

ASSEMBLED PLANE

all dimensions are millimetres (mm)

Steam-roller

Materials required

1 cylinder of pine (or deal) 80 mm × 57 mm diameter

1 piece of pine (or deal) 120 × 60 × 35 mm

1 piece of pine (or deal) 150 × 70 × 24 mm

1 piece of pine (or deal) 210 × 105 × 20 mm

1 piece of beech 100 × 55 × 55 mm

1 piece of 6 mm plywood 160 × 70 mm

550 mm length of 6-mm diameter dowel rod

220 mm length of 9-mm diameter dowel rod

25 mm length of 12-mm diameter dowel rod

1 piece of 9 mm plywood (grade 1) 125 × 100 mm

Small quantity of resin 'W' glue

Model-size tins of enamels, various colours

Joining the body to the roller

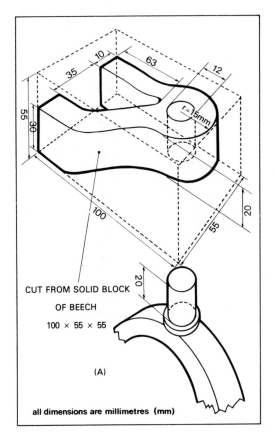

CUT FROM SOLID BLOCK
OF BEECH
100 × 55 × 55

(A)

all dimensions are millimetres (mm)

This toy is made of a number of different woods, according to the stress each part must bear. The rectangular frame (100 × 80 mm) and semi-circular mounting for the roller are made from a sheet of grade 1 plywood, 9 mm thick. The semi-circular mounting is cut out from the piece of plywood removed from the inside of the frame. A mortise and tenon joint is used to attach the 12-mm diameter wooden pivot to the semi-circular mounting. This pivot is designed to turn in a hole drilled in the bearing block attached to the front end of the boiler. This bearing block (diagram A) is shaped from a block of beech 100 × 55 × 55 mm. Better and more accurate results will be achieved if the 12-mm diameter hole is drilled in the rectangular block before any shaping is attempted. If, upon assembly, the 12-mm diameter pivot will not quite go into the 12-mm diameter hole, use a medium glasspaper on the pivot until a fairly tight fit is achieved. The roller is made from a piece of pine or deal, 57 mm in diameter and 80 mm long. It rotates on a piece of 6-mm diameter dowel rod.

Softwood (pine or deal) is quite suitable for most of the remaining parts. The boiler is shaped from a block measuring 120 × 60 × 35 mm, the front being shaped into a 'V' with an apex angle of about 140°. It is screwed to the base, which measures 150 × 70 × 24 mm, from underneath. The large wheels are 83 mm in diameter and 20 mm thick. They rotate on an axle made from 9-mm diameter dowel rod, cut to a length of 120 mm. The funnel is made from a piece of 9-mm diameter dowel rod, 50 mm long.

Made from 6 mm plywood, the roof measures 150 × 70 mm. The four uprights are made from lengths of dowel rod, each 6 mm in diameter and 113 mm long; 10 mm is let into holes in the base and 3 mm into holes in the roof, giving a clearance of 100 mm.

If you wish to paint or varnish the steam-roller, you will find it easier to do this before gluing the component parts together. Owing to the stress put upon it, it would be advisable to use four 25 mm panel pins in the wings of the bearing block where it is glued to the front of the boiler (diagram B).

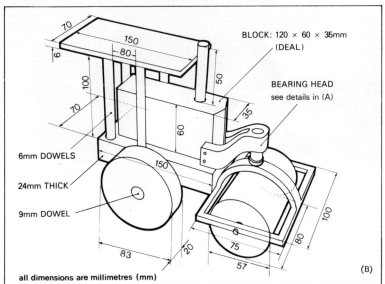

BLOCK: 120 × 60 × 35mm
(DEAL)

BEARING HEAD
see details in (A)

6mm DOWELS

24mm THICK

9mm DOWEL

all dimensions are millimetres (mm)

(B)

Train

Material required per wagon

1 piece of pine (or deal) 100 × 45 × 18 mm
350 mm length of 6-mm diameter dowel rod
2 wooden beads, 15 mm diameter
30 mm length of broom handle or 30-mm diameter dowel rod
4 domed chair nails
1 piece of 3 mm plywood 110 × 15 mm
1 cylinder of pine (or deal) 80 mm × 40 mm diameter
1 cylinder of pine (or deal) 50 mm × 30 mm diameter
1 half-cylinder of pine (or deal) 40 mm × 40 mm diameter
1 piece of pine (or deal) 40 × 40 × 20 mm
8 pieces of pine (or deal) 120 × 25 × 6 mm
4 fibre washers with 8-mm diameter centre holes
Model-size tins of enamels, various colours

This small train is made of a variable number of parts. You can have two, three or four wagons, depending on your materials and patience! They all follow the same general pattern; only the detachable pieces vary.

The basic structure is formed by a small rectangular block (100 × 43 × 18 mm) with two holes drilled for the axles. The axles (6 mm dowel) are 62 mm long and the distance between the wheel centres is 58 mm. The plywood wheels are 30 mm in diameter and 6 mm thick. The wheels are attached to the axles by chair-nails, with a fibre washer either side of each wheel. Two vertical shafts, capped by a ball, pass through the detachable pieces and hold them in place on the base by fitting tightly into two holes (8 mm deep). These shafts are 6 mm in diameter and 65 mm long. The holes in the base are drilled 40 mm apart. The coupling system is very simple: it is a small plank (105 × 14 × 3 mm) with two holes drilled 80 mm apart (from centre to centre). The shafts of two different wagons pass through these holes.

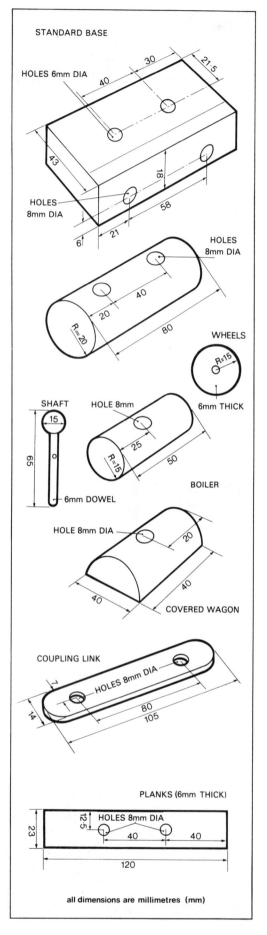

Sealing

Tracing

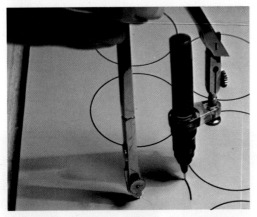

Drawing with a Rapidograph

Applying transfers

Wheel of fortune

Materials required

1 piece of 18 mm chipboard 400 × 280 mm
1 piece of 12 mm chipboard 280 × 200 mm
1 piece of 9 mm plywood 290 mm square
1 piece of 6 mm plywood 220 × 140 mm
40 mm length of 9-mm diameter dowel rod
2 fibre washers to fit over 9-mm diameter dowel rod
1 domed chair nail
40 mm length 3-mm diameter plastic rod (or plastic knitting needle)
50 × 15-mm large-headed brass decorative nails
Various transfers
Small quantity of resin 'W' glue
Model-size tins of enamels, various colours

The two main parts of this wheel of fortune are made out of chipboard. Each surface has to be very carefully prepared because chipboard is not smooth enough without preparation to be decorated in any way. However, chipboard has the advantage of being much cheaper than solid wood.

The base is 18 mm thick, 398 mm long and 279 mm wide. Make a groove 60 mm from one end, 8 mm deep and as wide as the upright panel is thick (12 mm). Mark the groove with two saw cuts to make the chiselling easier. Make an axle for the wheel 35 mm long from 9 mm diameter beech dowel and push the axle into a hole drilled 140 mm up the 12 mm-thick vertical panel. The big wheel, made of plywood, is 280 mm in diameter and 9 mm thick. The central hole has to be enlarged slightly so that the wheel can spin freely. To avoid any friction, place a small protective washer over the axle against the vertical panel. The central figure is cut out of 6 mm plywood and is held in place with a chair nail. Check the fit of all parts after they have been sealed.

The surfaces are prepared with a thick coating of wood-grain filler which you spread with a spatula, having first applied a coat of primer (any colour will do, so finish off your old tins). Glass-paper the whole surface to remove any rough patches before applying the top coat which will give the toy its final colour.

The coating and lacquering will allow you to choose any type of decoration: paints, collages, transfers, inks, etc. We have combined several techniques. The rectangles and circles are done with a compass or Rapidograph. The coloured figures and the borders are done with transfers. The central figure is painted with enamels.

Blending the paints

N.B. Blend the colours thoroughly in a shaker before applying them. It is rare to find a shop which stocks all the shades you want, so some colours must be mixed – pink, for example (pink = red + brown + white). Wait until each colour is dry before applying the next. Always start with the lightest colour and finish with the darkest. You can correct a smudge or a line which goes astray by wiping very gently with a clean rag dipped in white spirit, which is also handy for thinning paint or cleaning your brushes. You can purchase a wide range of coloured adhesive films, which will simplify your choice of colours.

On this model we have arranged the identical colours so that they are opposite each other on the wheel, which has 24 squares around the circumference and 12 circles around the inner ring. These designs are reproduced on the base.

You can find any number of transfers on all sorts of themes. Apply them with a spatula, a special applicator or the cap of a ball-point pen. You can also cut figures out of newspapers and glue them on. It is advisable to cover these collages with a special varnish.

Place the nails very carefully. Do not knock them in too close to the edge of the wheel or the chipboard will split. The flexible clicker is glued into a notch in the base; it should be made of a thin plastic rod about 30 mm long and 3 mm in diameter.

The rules of the game are very simple. The players bet in turn by placing their tokens on the base in the square or circle of their choice. The wheel turns and indicates the winning figure. If the wheel stops at a star, all the stakes are automatically lost and the bank takes all.

Slotting in the upright

Hole for the striker

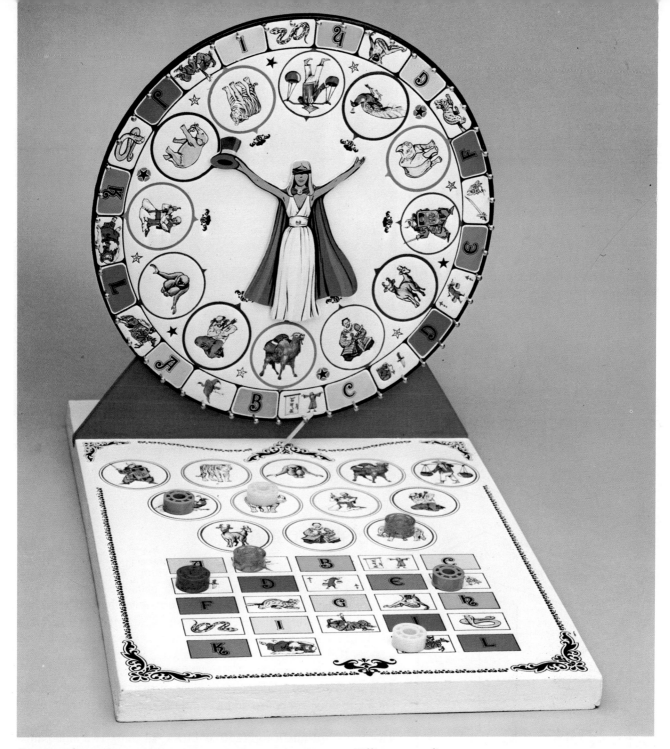

Spacing the nails

Filling any splits

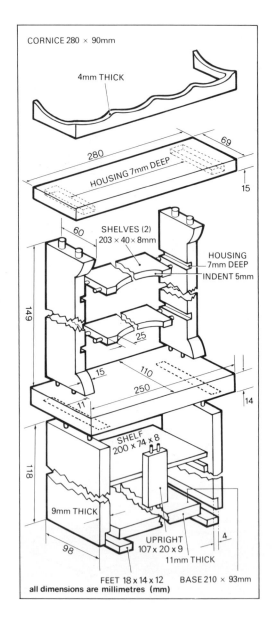

CORNICE 280 × 90mm
4mm THICK
280
69
HOUSING 7mm DEEP
15
60
SHELVES (2)
203 × 40 × 8mm
HOUSING
7mm DEEP
INDENT 5mm
149
25
15
110
250
14
11
SHELF
200 × 74 × 8
118
9mm THICK
98
UPRIGHT
107 × 20 × 9
4
11mm THICK
FEET 18 × 14 × 12   BASE 210 × 93mm
all dimensions are millimetres (mm)

Welsh dresser

This is a beautiful example of scorching with a blow-lamp. Resinous woods are the most suitable because of their special texture which gives a very attractive decorative finish. The technique brings out very effectively the grain of such woods (especially pine), whereas it would cause other woods simply to blacken all over. N.B. Keep the flame low or the wood will catch fire!

This small dresser is a charming piece of rustic furniture comprising a two-door cupboard and a china rack with two shelves.

The cupboard has a top (250 × 110 × 14 mm), two side-panels (118 × 9 × 98 mm), two doors (95 × 105 × 6 mm) hinged on their ends with 3-mm dowels top and bottom, an upright (107 × 20 × 9 mm) against which the doors close, a base (210 × 93 × 11 mm) which fits 4 mm into the side-panels, a plywood backing panel (200 × 124 × 6 mm), a shelf (200 × 74 × 9 mm), two brackets (70 × 6 × 4 mm) supporting the shelf, and four feet cut out of two cross-pieces (80 × 14 × 12 mm).

The two uprights of the china rack are 149 × 60 × 15 mm; they have a 14 mm deep indentation. The two shelves (203 × 40 × 8 mm) fit 7 mm into each upright. They have a 5 mm indentation along 153 mm of their front edge. The backing panel (203 × 148 × 6 mm) is plywood. The 4 mm-thick cornice runs around three sides of the top (280 × 69 × 15 mm). All the joints are reinforced by glued dowels.

Bed

For reasons of sturdiness it was necessary to make this little bed entirely of oak, which is not only attractive to look at but also easy to cut accurately. Beech or ash could also be used. It was not possible to make the pieces from plywood because their small size does not allow much margin for trimming.

The four posts (100 mm at the head and 60 mm at the foot) are made from 15 × 15 mm. The side-members (178 mm) and the cross-members (96 mm) are cut from a 9-mm thick sheet. The bars (56 and 55 mm at the head and 24 mm at the foot) are cut from 5 × 5 mm. The lattice base (182 × 100 mm) is made from 5 × 6 mm moulding using cross-halving joints, as are the two supports glued to the inside of the side-members. The posts are assembled with glued dowels, while the bars are fitted by mortise.

Assembling the base with cross-halving joints

Toy chest

This beautiful chest is also made of oak. The base is 157 × 54 × 3 mm. All the 10 mm square members are assembled with glued dowels. The side-members measure 157 mm, the cross-members 54 mm and the uprights 98 mm. The panels are 6 mm thick and 70 mm high. The reliefs added to the panels are 2 mm thick. With a chisel, make a rectangular groove around the top of the cover (7 mm thick) and glue to its underside a sheet of wood which will ensure that the top fits squarely on the chest: a rectangular piece of plywood 3 mm thick and the same size as the internal measurements of the chest.

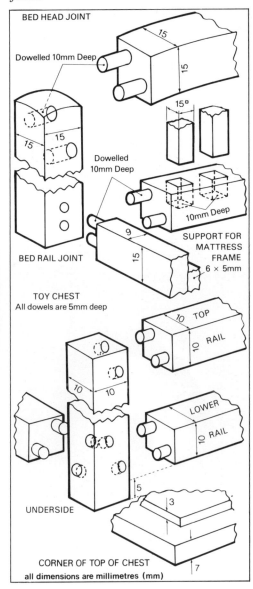

BED HEAD JOINT

Dowelled 10mm Deep

15

15

15°

Dowelled 10mm Deep

10mm Deep

BED RAIL JOINT

9

15

SUPPORT FOR MATTRESS FRAME 6 × 5mm

TOY CHEST
All dowels are 5mm deep

TOP

10

RAIL

10

10

10

LOWER

RAIL

10

5

UNDERSIDE

3

CORNER OF TOP OF CHEST

7

all dimensions are millimetres (mm)

Fixing the head with glue and nails

Caterpillar

Materials required

1 broom head with bristles
1 ball, approximate diameter 100 mm, made of wood, rubber or plastic
1 strip of strong canvas or thin leather, 500 × 60 mm
Quantity of 12-mm tin-tacks
Small quantity of resin 'W' glue
Model-size tins of enamels, various colours

Make a caterpillar from a broom? Yes, it's perfectly possible – see for yourself. Of course, it's a very large caterpillar, but don't worry, it won't eat your lettuces. It is completely harmless and very easy-going.

It is the ideal playmate for small children, who will spend hour after hour making it creep and crawl through the fantasy world of their imagination. An evil spirit one moment, a friendly monster with magic powers the next, this remarkable caterpillar will take on all sorts of personalities in their eyes.

Cut its seven sections from a suitable broom head after first planing flat the part into which the handle is inserted. Take care to saw very steadily between the tufts as far as the staples which hold the bristles. Cut the staples with a metal hacksaw. If any bristles fall out, fill the holes carefully. The head is made from a ball of about 100 mm in diameter. It will be easier to fix the head to the base if you plane off a millimetre or so to make a small flat. Cut out a strip of flexible material (strong canvas, thin leather, etc.) 500 mm long and 58 mm wide and pointed at each end. Decorate the caterpillar before you glue and pin the pieces to the strip, about 25 mm apart.

Spray-paint, enamels and coloured adhesive films together produce an attractive effect

1 *2* *3*

Materials required
1 broom – head + handle
1 piece of 6 mm plywood
300 × 150 mm
Various wooden beads,
15 – 20 mm diameter
Various flat-headed round nails,
12 – 30 mm long
Small quantity of resin 'W' glue
Model-size tins of enamels,
various colours

Funny faces

All sorts of unusual objects and figures can be fashioned from broom heads. The funny faces illustrated here offer only a glimpse of the many creative possibilities presented by the unique features of brushes, brooms, hand-brushes, etc. Any type of broom can be used to make these head-shaped toys. Happy, sad or enigmatic, they can reflect all moods.

1. Follow the instructions for the caterpillar. The main piece (58 × 30 × 17 mm) is taken from the head of a broom with the bristles left intact. Do this by sawing carefully between the rows of bristles. The eyes are circles (10 mm thick) cut from the broom-handle and drilled through the centre. Nail them in place.

2. This face is made from two sections of a broom glued together on their flat sides. For the ears and the nose, cut sections of the handle in two. The eyes are made by gluing beads to more handle sections.

3. For this face, take the two ends of the broom head and assemble them as in the photo. The nose, tongue, eyebrows and eyes are made from sections of broom handle: quarter, half, half and whole respectively, plus two wooden beads for the eyes. Glue a piece of plywood at the back for reinforcement, and pin the eyebrows to this through the bristles.

4. This face is made from similar pieces to the three others, except that it is reinforced at the back with a sheet of plywood.

4

Simple rocking-horse

Assembling the components

Materials required

1 piece of 18 mm birch plywood 950 × 600 mm
Quantity of marine-quality clear varnish

This rocking-horse is much smaller than the one shown on page 42. It is intended for younger children and so is no more than 350 mm high and 575 mm long.

It is made from 18 mm thick birch multi-ply and comprises only four parts, two of which – the side-panels – are identical. These have two 19 mm wide slots set in line 100 mm apart; the first is 140 mm long, the second 60 mm long. The three angles formed by the edges of these pieces are 38°, 155° and 108° respectively. The smallest angle is rounded, as are all the edges of the toy's four parts. The arc of the rocker follows a 1500 mm diameter circle.

The cross-piece is symmetrical; a piece is cut out on either side of its axis to leave two unequal projections which slot into the side-panels. Note that the top projection has two 50 mm diameter holes which the child can grasp, and that the lower projection serves as a foot-rest. The central hole, which is made 90 mm from the top edge, receives the tenon of the seat. Two deep, narrow slots made on either side of the tenon hold all four parts firmly together.

Assembly is simple. Slot the two side-panels onto the cross-piece and then fix the seat in place by slotting the tenon into the hole.

CONSTRUCTED FROM 18mm PLYWOOD

HOLE 50mm DIA

all dimensions are millimetres (mm)

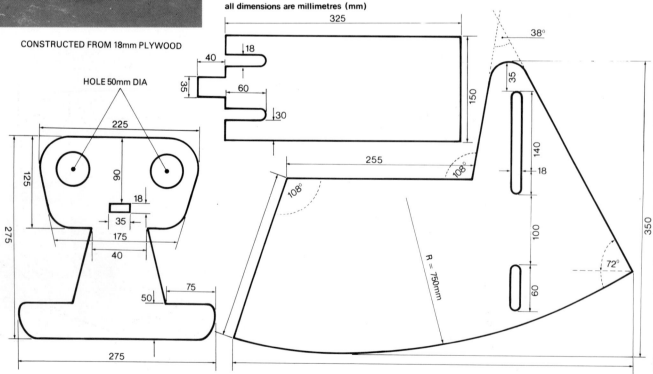

Adaptable units

Materials required

1 piece of 18 mm beech plywood 750 × 580 mm
2 × 600 mm lengths of 9-mm diameter dowel rod
4 × 410 mm lengths of 24-mm diameter dowel rod
8 fibre washers to fit over 24-mm diameter dowel rod
Small quantity of resin 'W' glue
$\frac{1}{4}$ litre of marine varnish

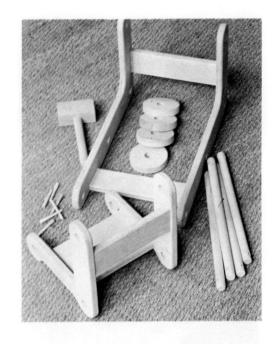

The great advantage of these modular units is that they can be assembled in different ways according to the use to which they are to be put; they can be turned into a cart, a small table, a push-chair, etc. Their logical and beautifully proportioned design is highly adaptable.

Most of the dimensions have been chosen in multiples of 70 mm, this being the full width of the straight members. It is made from 18 mm beech multi-ply. As with certain hard woods, this invests all the parts with very good mechanical properties, especially axial compression. In addition, beech is an easy wood to work. It can be varnished, stained or left natural. In each case, all surfaces and edges must be carefully sanded.

The larger unit has two L-shaped side-pieces 70 mm in width. The long side measures 490 mm and the short side 280 mm. Their corners are all rounded following the curve of a 70-mm diameter circle centred on the hole for the cross-bars. Two flat spacers keep the distance between the side-pieces constant. They are fixed to the outer edge of the side-pieces, 70 mm from the ends, with 9-mm diameter dowel glued in place. (Length of the spacers: 250 mm; width of the upper spacer: 70 mm; width of the lower spacer: 140 mm.)

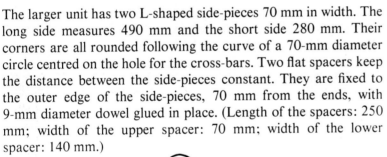

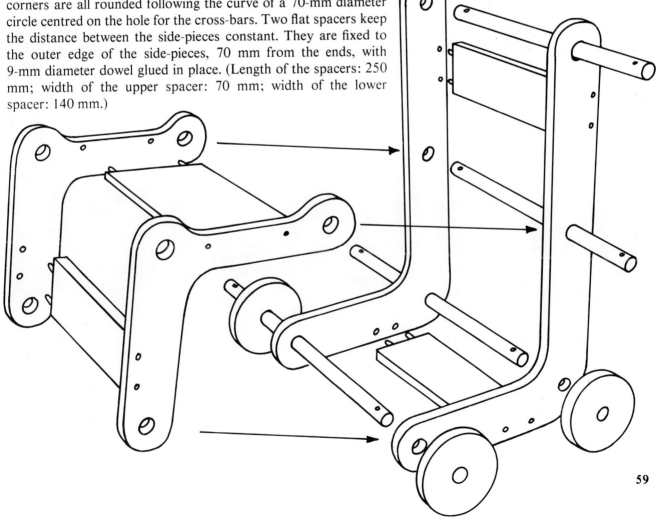

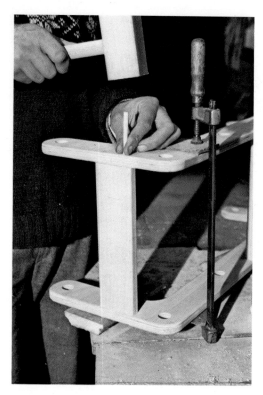

Inserting the dowel-pins in the cross-members

Four 24-mm diameter holes are made along the axis of the large L-shaped side-pieces, equally spaced at intervals of 210 mm.

The smaller unit is also L-shaped, the only differences being that both its sides are the same length (280 mm) and that the middle section of one of the outer edges is indented (width at this point: 50 mm). Each side has three 24-mm diameter holes situated at the ends and at the angle of the L. Two flat spacers similar to those of the larger unit keep the two side-pieces parallel. They are positioned close to the outer edges and are 210 mm long, which means that this unit will fit inside the larger one. The spacer at the indentation is 140 mm wide, while the other spacer is 70 mm wide; remember that they are both fixed to the outer edge of the L-piece with dowels glued in place.

Four circular cross-bars are used to assemble the two units. These bars are 24 mm in diameter and have two holes (340 mm apart centre to centre) to take the draw-pins (9 mm in diameter and 50 mm long) holding them in place. There are 8 of them, thus making numerous combinations possible. In the chair, for example, the two L-shaped units are assembled head to tail so that the long sides of the larger unit are vertical and the small unit is turned upside down with the large spacer uppermost.

The two bottom ends of the small unit are fitted to the ends of the short sides of the big unit by means of the bars, while the two top ends are fitted to the middle hole in the long sides of the big L. In this assembly the bottom bars both have two wheels 105 mm in diameter fixed to their ends inside the draw-pins (diameter of the axle hole: 24 mm). Plastic or fibre washers should be used either side of each wheel. All the draw-pins and axles must have their ends rounded for safety.

Climbing frame

Basic see-saw

Slide, see-saw and climbing frame

Materials required

1 sheet of 18 mm beech plywood 2400 × 1200 mm
2 pieces of 18 mm beech plywood 225 × 150 mm
3 × 1-metre lengths of 24-mm diameter dowel rod
1 piece of 24 mm plywood 1200 × 40 mm for the square wooden nuts
2 × 1-metre lengths of 9-mm diameter dowel rod
$\frac{1}{4}$ litre of marine varnish

This model can be adapted to a great many uses. We will just mention here the basic see-saw (when the biggest unit is placed with its rounded edge on the ground), the see-saw with support (when the large triangle is placed over it in order, among other things, to limit the rocking by the fact that its bottom ends extend beyond the rounded base of the see-saw), the slide (when one end of the see-saw is fixed to the apex of the triangle, which serves as a ladder) and the climbing frame (the children can climb in and out of the five bars of the triangular structure).

All parts are cut out of an 18 mm thick sheet of beech multi-ply 1200 × 2400 mm. All faces must be carefully sanded to avoid

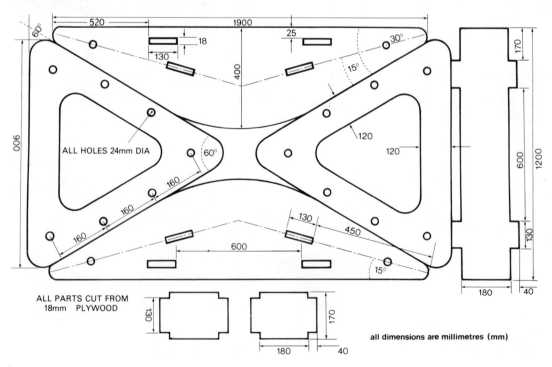

ALL HOLES 24mm DIA

ALL PARTS CUT FROM
18mm PLYWOOD

all dimensions are millimetres (mm)

any accidents due to splinters and all edges must be rounded as an additional safety precaution. Draw the cutting plan as accurately as possible on the wood to obtain the most economical use of your raw materials. In theory, you should be able to cut the three pieces of the see-saw and the two sides of the triangular structure from the same sheet of wood.

The two sides of the see-saw-cum-slide are very elongated, with two 30° rounded corners and a length of 1900 mm. Two 130 mm slots are made 90 mm from the long edge to receive the tenons of the seat plank, which is 650 mm wide. Another two slots receive the tenons of the lower cross-pieces. These are cut along the line bisecting the angle of the top corners of the panels, as also are two circular holes (24 mm in diameter). The holes enable the two units to be joined together. Two more holes made on either side of the median axis of the panels allow the two units to be fixed together in the see-saw position, by means of the cross-bars.

The second unit is made of two open triangular panels joined by 7 round dowel cross-bars (24 mm in diameter) in addition to the two bars which attach the slide to the triangle. As shown in the photographs, the bars (278 mm long) are fixed in place with 40-mm square wooden nuts made from 24 mm plywood. A shoulder is made at each end of the dowel, and the narrower part is threaded to take the nuts. However, this requires a special threading device, not easily obtainable. An alternative method is to hold the unthreaded nuts in place and to drill through nut and dowel from the side, to take a wooden pin. The protruding ends of the pin can then be cut away.

If a shoulder is not cut in the dowel, two wooden nuts should be used at each end, one either side of the triangular panel.

Slide

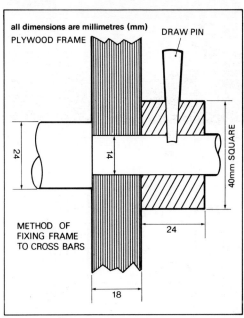

Fixing the frame to the cross-bars: shouldered dowel with nut fixed by pin

See-saw and support

Scooter

Materials required

1 piece of good, straight-grained pine 1500 × 80 × 50 mm
650 mm length of 24-mm diameter dowel rod
250 mm length of 9-mm dowel rod
3 carriage bolts (with nuts), 10 mm diameter and 90 mm long
3 steel washers to fit over 10 mm bolts
8 fibre washers to fit over 24-mm diameter dowel rods
1 piece of 24 mm plywood 430 × 110 mm
$\frac{1}{4}$ litre of marine varnish

The two main parts of this scooter are cut from a 50 × 80 mm length of pine. They are both 700 mm long, with chamfered edges and rounded corners. The vertical part has a neck which is cut out with a saw and chisel and finished with a file. The neck is cylindrical and is 33 mm in diameter. It is 70 mm from the bottom end and fits into the horizontal platform, which is made from two identical parts. Each part has a semi-circular hole carved out, slightly larger in diameter than the neck. The hole formed by the parts is thus in the centre of the platform. The two pieces are separated by washers to allow the head to move, and held together with three bolts.

A hole 25 mm in diameter is drilled in the flat face of the upright, 20 mm from its bottom end. This hole takes the axle (24 mm in diameter and 160 mm long) on which the wheels turn (105 mm in diameter and 24 mm thick). They are secured with rounded draw-pins 9 mm in diameter and 50 mm long. The gap between the draw-pin holes (centre to centre) is 170 mm. The rear wheels are the same size and are assembled in similar fashion, 100 mm from the end of the platform. The rear axle is 170 mm long. All the wheels should have plastic or fibre washers either side.

The handle is formed by a piece of dowel 24 mm in diameter and 300 mm long. It is fitted into a hole through the upright 20 mm from the top.

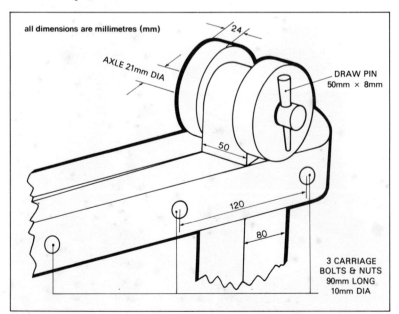